Tales Behind
the Tombstones

Tales Behind the Tombstones

*The Deaths and Burials of the Old West's Most
Nefarious Outlaws, Notorious Women,
and Celebrated Lawmen*

Chris Enss

TWODOT®

GUILFORD, CONNECTICUT
HELENA, MONTANA
AN IMPRINT OF ROWMAN & LITTLEFIELD

A · TWODOT® · BOOK

Copyright © 2007 Rowman & Littlefield

TwoDot is a registered trademark of Rowman & Littlefield.

Distributed by NATIONAL BOOK NETWORK

Library of Congress Cataloging-in-Publication Data is available.
ISBN 978-0-7627-3773-4

Printed in the United States of America

For my friend Chris Navo

Contents

Acknowledgments

Without the assistance from numerous historical societies, museums, and the staff at cemeteries from Oregon to Kansas, this publication would not have been possible.

I would like to thank the eager personnel at the Denver Library, the Library of Congress, and the Allegheny Cemetery in Pittsburgh, Pennsylvania. Chrystal Carpenter Burke at the Arizona Historical Society was a delight to work with, as was Doug Miller at the Ross Bay Cemetery in Victoria, British Columbia. Michael Sinnwell with Rocky Mountain Profiles, Shelley Howe at the Buffalo Bill Museum and Grave, and Peggy Wood at the Masonic Cemetery in Las Cruces, New Mexico, went out of their way to provide photographs to use in this publication.

I appreciate the contributions made by the El Dorado County Museum in Placerville, California, the South Dakota Historical Society in Deadwood, South Dakota, and the Nevada Historical Society in Reno, Nevada. Ed Tyson at the Searls Library in Nevada City, California, offered invaluable insight and was always willing to dig for more information and pictures on the requested subjects. Thank you to Sister Kathleen Padden at the Ursuline Convent of the Sacred Heart in Toledo, Ohio, for your prompt response on Mary Fields. Thanks to the researchers at the California State Library, John Doerner at the Little Bighorn Battlefield Museum, and the rangers at the Bodie State Park in Bodie, California.

And finally, thanks to Erin Turner and the art department at Globe Pequot Press. I never cease to be amazed at the quality of work you do or the talent you possess. As a lover of Old West history, I was pleased to be given the chance to write about how trailblazers such as Carrie Nation, Mary Fields, and James Marshall left this world.

Introduction

"A cemetery is a history of people—a perpetual record of yesterday and sanctuary of peace and quiet today. A cemetery exists because every life is worth loving and remembering—always."
— WILLIAM GLADSTONE,
PRIME MINISTER OF ENGLAND, 1890

In the mid-1800s courageous pioneers ventured across the rugged plains to start a new life. The weathered tombstones and worn-out crosses that dot the trails from Independence, Missouri, to San Francisco, California, represent the brave souls who passed away traveling across the wild frontier. Many who made the arduous journey died from disease, starvation, or the inhospitable elements in an unfamiliar land. Some died violent deaths from gunfights and lawlessness often associated with the untamed West.

Emigrants were often too busy with day-to-day survival to spend the time and effort to create cemeteries. Family members and friends were buried where they fell. Most of the headboards of Indian scouts, wagon masters, business owners, soldiers, women, prospectors, and children have since toppled over, and in some cases all that remains is a sun-scorched piece of wood teetering on the edge of a grave.

The gravesites of the men and women who conquered the western frontier more than 150 years ago offer important reminders of that famous era. Even those headboards containing only a name and date spark a curiosity in visitors strolling quietly through the cemeteries of old. Many of the markers that still stand and are still legible often don't tell the story of the remarkable, dedicated, outrageous, and sometimes notorious people who made a lasting impression conquering the new frontier.

In many cases the manner of their deaths and odd details of their impromptu funerals are as interesting as the lives they led. For example, many people have seen Buffalo Bill Cody's grave on Lookout Mountain in Golden, Colorado, but many do not know that shortly after Cody's death the governor of the state dispatched a World War I tank to the site to protect his remains.

Whether or not they were famous, how pioneers were treated after they passed is worthy of note. Settlers who died on the trek west were generally wrapped in material or blankets and then buried. The wooden flanks that lined the bottom of wagons were occasionally used to make crude caskets. Rocks were piled high over the grave to prevent wild animals from getting to the remains. Surviving settlers rolled wagons over the top of the graves to conceal the plots from vengeful Indians. Family members drove away from the burial site with particularly heavy hearts. Not only had they lost a loved one, but the chance that they would ever be able to find and visit the burial site again was slim.

When western towns such as Sacramento, Tucson, and Denver were established, graveyards and proper burials became standard. Coffins were made with rough boards and lined with white cloths. In small mining burgs, friends and family carried the coffin to the cemetery. In larger towns the casket was placed in a black, horse-drawn vehicle complete with glass sides and decorated with elaborate carvings and brass ornaments. The deceased was driven to his final resting place by a team of six horses. A member of the clergy would offer a few words about the departed and lead those gathered in prayer.

The undertaker usually made the wooden markers placed at the graves. Granite or marble tombstones had to be ordered from such major cities as Kansas City, San Francisco, or Denver, and the inscriptions were scrawled across the front before they were sent back to the families. The process took three to six months to complete. From time to time the stone would be returned with the name misspelled or key information omitted. Given the cost and time spent, the stone was used regardless of the mistake.

In absence of centralized death records in the Old West, tombstones are the lingering evidence that a person once was. Included in this volume are locations of these markers and little-known particulars of the deaths and burials. The tales included here are meant to encourage history buffs to visit these final resting places and consider them as frontier landmarks. In the case of Sheriff David Douglass, they will not only be standing at the grave of a gold rush hero but also standing on the spot of his last gunfight.

Included in this volume are a few of the interesting tombstone inscriptions, unusual burial places, and strange circumstances surrounding some well-known western heroes and frontier characters. While there are many compelling tales behind the tombstones, the headboards included in this guide were chosen as the most fascinating and least told.

Many visitors standing over the burial plots of such legends as Lotta Crabtree, Doc Holliday, and Lola Montez, or lesser known pioneers such as Old Joe or Sheriff David Douglass wonder where the occupants of the graves were when they met their maker, their course of death, or who witnessed their last words. *Tales Behind the Tombstones* answers those queries and serves as a guide through the hallowed grounds where today one can visit the markers of pioneers, bad guys, missionaries, teamsters, entertainers, and lawmen of the Old West.

Juanita

d. 1851

*"About 10 o'clock in the morning of July 5, 1851, the cry
of 'murder!' came up the river. Everybody was running
toward town. At the scene of the action we found a vast
throng surrounding a clapboard shanty, and within, a
miner was lying dead."*

— A WITNESS ON THE SCENE IMMEDIATELY
AFTER THE KILLING OF FRED CANNON, 1851

The Fourth of July celebration held in Downieville, California, in
1851 was a festive event that included a parade, a picnic, and patri-
otic speeches from numerous politicians. Proud members of the
Democratic County Convention spoke to the cheering crowd of
more than five thousand people, primarily gold miners, about free-
dom and the idea that all are considered equal.

The celebration was accentuated with gambling at all the
local saloons and the consumption of alcohol, available in large
barrels lining the streets. When residents weren't listening to ora-
tors wax nostalgic, many happy and drunk souls gathered at Jack
Craycroft's Saloon to watch a dark-eyed beauty named Juanita deal
cards.

Juanita was from Sonora, Mexico, and engaged to the
saloon's bartender, but that did not stop amorous miners from

attempting to get close to her. Fred Cannon, a well-liked Scotsman who lived in town, frequently propositioned Juanita. On the Fourth of July in 1851, he took her usual rejection particularly hard and threatened to have his way with her regardless.

PHOTOGRAPH BY CYNTHIA MARTIN

Juanita's tombstone

When Juanita finished work that evening, she went straight home. The streets were still busy with rowdy patriots who weren't willing to stop celebrating. Fred Cannon was among the men on the thoroughfare who were drinking and firing their guns in the air. After more than a few beers, Fred decided to take the celebration to Juanita's house.

Juanita was preparing for bed when Fred pounded on the front of her home and suddenly burst in, knocking the door off the hinges. She yelled at the drunken man to get out. Before leaving, Fred cursed at her and threw some of her things on the floor. The following morning Juanita confronted Fred about his behavior and demanded he fix her door. He refused, insisting that the door was flimsy and was in danger of falling off the frame prior to his involvement. Juanita was enraged by his response, and the two argued bitterly. When Fred cursed at her this time, she pulled a knife on him and stabbed him in the chest.

Fred's friends surrounded the woman, calling her a harlot and a murderer. They demanded that she be hanged outright. Many of the townspeople insisted on trying her first, however. After a quick and biased hearing, Juanita was found guilty and sentenced to be hanged. The fearless woman held her head up as she was led to the spot where she would be put to death. She refused a blindfold, and when asked if she had any final words about the crime for which she was accused, she simply nodded her head. She boldly stated that she was not sorry and that she would "do it again if so provoked."

Juanita was the first woman to be hanged in the state of California. She was buried in the same grave as Fred Cannon. The pair was moved from the site six months later when gold was discovered where they laid. Their remains were relocated to the Downieville Cemetery. Time and the elements have erased the name of the infamous Juanita from the marker that stands over her grave.

The Brennan Family
d. 1858

"It is the saddest tragedy that has ever sustained the pages of the county's history."
— California Historian William Lardner's thoughts about the death of the Brennan Family, 1924

In 1849 San Francisco newspapers were read so thoroughly by excited citizens in the East that only scraps remained. Front pages were filled with encouraging words about a significant find at Sutter's Mill on the American River in California. "The streams are paved with gold," the report read, "the mountains swell in their golden girdle. It sparkles in the sand of the valleys, it glitters in the coronets of the steep cliffs." The news brought ambitious miners from all over the world to the area to get rich.

Michael Brennan, an Irishman from New York, arrived in the Gold Country in late 1850 determined to find the mother lode. The well-educated man convinced the management at the Mount Hope Mining Company in Grass Valley, California, that he had a gift for locating major gold veins. He was quickly hired and made the company's superintendent.

After moving his wife and children into a modest home near the mine, Brennan went to work. For two years Brennan and his

PHOTOGRAPH BY CYNTHIA MARTIN

The tombstone over the Brennan grave reads: MICHAEL AGED 38,
DORINDA AGED 32, ELLEN AGED 7, ROBERT AGED 5, DORINDA AGED 2.
DIED FEB. 21, 1858. NATIVES OF IRELAND

team of diggers searched for gold, but the rich strike eluded him.
He was racked with guilt over the money the mine owners had
invested in his efforts and believed he had disgraced his family in
the process.

On February 21, 1858, in a fit of melancholy and dejection,
Brennan decided to end the pain he was feeling. The suicide note
he wrote sadly stated "he could not bear to leave his family behind
living in poverty." Using prussic acid, he poisoned his wife and children and then himself. A pistol was found lying next to Brennan's
body along with the vile of poison. Authorities determined that he
had intended to shoot himself if the acid was not effective.

The entire family was laid to rest side by side at the Elm Ridge Cemetery in Grass Valley, California. A single marker listing the names and ages of all five Brennans covers the grave.

The Lone Grave
1858

It was the news of gold that let loose a flood of humanity upon the foothills of Northern California. Prior to 1849 most west-heading wagons were bound for Oregon. All at once settlers burst onto the scene searching for their fortune in gold. Some found what they hoped for, but others found nothing but tragedy. Such was the case for the Apperson family, pioneers who lost a young family member in a fiery accident in 1858.

The wagon train the sojourners were a part of struggled to make its way over the treacherous Sierra Nevadas and down the other side into the valley below. The Appersons and their fellow travelers were exhausted from the four-month overland trip, which had started in Independence, Missouri. After reaching the outskirts of the mining community of Nevada City, California, they made camp as usual and rested for a few days before moving the train on into town.

The forest settling was idyllic, and the Appersons decided to stay there instead of going on with the others. They built a home for themselves and their four children. For a while they were truly happy. But on May 6, 1858, an unfortunate accident occurred that left them devastated.

At their father's request the Apperson children were dutifully burning household debris when the youngest boy, barely two years old, wandered too close to the flames, and his pant leg caught fire.

His sister and brothers tried desperately to extinguish the flames but were unsuccessful. The boy's mother heard his frantic screams and hurried to her child. She smothered him with her dress and apron, and then quickly rushed him to a nearby watering trough and immersed his body.

The child's legs and sides were severely burned, but he survived. For a time it seemed as though his injuries might not be life threatening. The boy lingered for a month and then died. He was buried at the southwest corner of their property. The Apperson family stayed only a few months after his death and then moved on.

At the time of his passing, the grave was marked only by two small seedlings. Since then concerned neighbors and community leaders have taken an interest in the burial site, surrounding the small spot with a fence and a marker.

Motorists driving along U.S. Highway 20 from Nevada City frequently stop to visit the lone grave beside the road. It lies to one side of the interstate between two large cedars. A stone plaque now stands over the place where the child lies. Donated by the Native Sons of the Golden West, the plaque reads JULIUS ALBERT APPERSON, BORN JUNE 1855. DIED MAY 6, 1858. A PIONEER WHO CROSSED THE PLAIN TO CALIFORNIA WHO DIED AND WAS BURIED HERE.

The Emigrant Trail followed along the ridge and through Nevada City. The marking of this lone grave perpetuates the memory of all the lone graves throughout the state. Not only does the plaque signify the grave as a historic landmark, it stands as a symbol of sacrifice.

Bodie's Odd Fellows Cemetery
Founded 1859

"Show me your cemeteries, and I will tell you what kind of people you have."
—BENJAMIN FRANKLIN (1706–1790)

For thousands of pioneers, the journey west was deadly. In 1875 gold miner P. Walhcim wrote in his journal, "If the graves of the early settlers who died on the pilgrimage across the great plains into the wild frontier had been marked, one could have traveled the entire distance stepping on a gravestone with each stride."

The cemetery in the ghost town of Bodie, California, is filled with the graves of immigrants who came in search of a better way of life in the so-called "utopian west." Disease claimed the lives of several interred there. Many others died from mining accidents or gunfights or perished in fires. Historical records disclose superficial facts about the untimely deaths of those prospectors and home-steaders and their families. Their loves, hopes, hates, joys, and sorrows faded away when they passed on.

Bodie was one of the most notorious gold boomtowns in the Old West. Founded in 1859 by William S. Bodey, who discovered gold at the location, the find attracted thousands to the area north of Mono Lake. By 1865 the town's population numbered more than ten thousand and included three general stores, six restaurants, a tin shop, a shoemaker business, and sixty-five saloons. The gold quartz mine around which the wild burg was situated yielded $75 million before being completely played out.

In addition to law-abiding citizens who lived and worked in Bodie were numerous bad men. Gunfights were commonplace and crime was rampant. The local newspaper, the *Bodie Daily Free Press*, featured a section entitled "Last Night's Killings," which listed the lives lost in various violent scrapes. The lawless atmosphere and frequent gunplay earned the rowdy community the nickname "Shooter's Town."

The citizens who permanently reside at the crowded cemetery came from all walks of life. The upstanding and commonly perceived as respected residents were laid to rest in the main portion of the graveyard. Soiled doves, drug addicts, bandits, and murderers were placed in the outcast section just beyond the gates of the main grounds.

Some of the people buried in the "proper" area of the cemetery were escorted to their final resting place by horse-drawn carriages and brass bands. When the bones of the town's founder were discovered in a spot near his initial mining claim, a lavish funeral followed. He was led to the graveyard in a massive black hearse pulled by a pair of plumed horses.

In late 1880 the death of a popular member of the Chinese Masonic Lodge prompted his friends to arrange for a grand send-off. The end result was a chaotic and tragic adventure that made the San Francisco newspapers.

The Bodie band, decked out in uniforms complete with military-style dress hats and plumes, marched in front of the casket as it was carried to the cemetery. Several days of rain prior to the occasion had left the streets muddy. Adorned in black and wearing overshoes, the procession slogged through the ankle-deep muck.

As the musicians played a fitting dirge, mourners ran alongside the coffin distributing slips of red paper full of holes. According to Chinese custom, evil spirits had to pass through all the holes before they could gain access to the soul of the departed.

At the conclusion of the graveside ceremonies, the crowd that had gathered started its way back into town. The band followed behind the hearse playing "The Girl I Left behind Me." One of the horses pulling a carriage driven by a mourner who did not want to make the trip on foot became spooked by the drums and bolted away from the procession. The runaway vehicle charged over the rocky landscape, tossing the driver and passengers to and fro. The funeral attendees raced after the out-of-control carriage hoping for a chance to intervene. The coach sped down the main street of town, nearly tipping over as it rounded a corner, and throwing the passengers off in the process. The vehicle was finally brought to a stop by a giant log in the roadway. The front wheel hit the timber, and the entire rig careened over. In the aftermath of the event, three people were left dead and several others were seriously injured.

Time has erased the inscriptions from many of the tombstones in the cemetery at Bodie. Only a few markers are left with any indication as to who the inhabitants were, how they died, and when. Partial information listed on select granite stones contains poems or Bible verses. The marker on the grave of a nameless woman who passed away in 1882 reads AMIABLE, SHE WON ALL. INTELLIGENT, SHE CHARMED ALL. FERVENT, SHE LOVED ALL. AND DYING SHE SADDENED ALL.

The tombstone over W. S. Bodey's grave doesn't include his name either. It reads SACRED TO THE MEMORY OF JAMES A. GARFIELD. In the midst of carving a sentiment on Bodey's stone, the sculptor was informed that President Garfield had been assassinated.

Shocked by the news and confused by the loss, the thoughtful inscription was etched.

Among the known individuals that reside at Bodie's Odd Fellows Cemetery are miners who lost their lives on the job. Swedish-born Alex Larson rests next to his coworker Norman McSwain. Larson survived an explosion at the mine that claimed the life of McSwain in July 1881. A few weeks after the blast, Larson fell backwards into an ore car and fell two hundred feet down a steep incline.

Tombstones containing the names of various children who died are scattered throughout the burial grounds. The marker over Nathan Cook Gregory's plot reads SUFFER LITTLE CHILD TO COME UNTO ME AND FORBID THEM NOT, FOR OF SUCH IS THE KINGDOM OF HEAVEN.

Murder victims such as Thomas Treloar reside at the cemetery as well, but his tombstone is too weathered to read. He was killed by his wife's lover when confronted with the affair. The man shot Treloar in the head at point-blank range and fled the area. He was apprehended seven days later eight miles outside of town and hanged.

Antone Valencia was shot down on Main Street by Jesus Revis after stabbing Jesus in the chest over a financial matter. Valencia died a few hours after having received the fatal wound. Both men were buried in the cemetery.

In mid-December 1881 a gruesome mystery led authorities to search the plot of Mary Turner, a nineteen-year-old woman interred at the graveyard. The young bride had died on December 9, and her grieving husband had her laid to rest close to W. S. Bodey's burial spot. Unbeknownst to him, and the majority of the townsfolk, her body had been exhumed by a local doctor and dissected.

After the macabre physician had completed the procedure, he dropped the remains in a mine shaft. A night watchman discovered the body and alerted the sheriff. The offense was traced back to a Doctor Blackwood. His office was searched and the woman's skull

PHOTOGRAPH BY CYNTHIA MARTIN

Many Bodie residents held funerals for family and friends at the Methodist Church. The classic structure is now closed to visitors. Vandals stole many of the interior ornaments, including an oilcloth imprinted with the Ten Comandments.

was found. Blackwood fled the area before he could be arrested and was never heard from again. Mary's remains were returned to her original grave.

Tombstones containing the names of prominent citizens stand beside Mary Turner's marker. Painter Lottie Johl rests in the main section of the cemetery. Lottie was married to Eli Johl, co-owner of one of Bodie's two butcher shops. The two met at a local dance hall where Lottie was one of the entertainers. Although her profession and past were questionable, Eli fell in love with her and the two wed.

Eli was able to see beyond Lottie's time spent as a divorced prostitute, but the prim and proper women in town could not. She was often the subject of scorn and ridicule. Eli showered his wife with gifts in spite of the criticism he took, and Lottie was grateful. She was left alone by her neighbors and the wives of her husband's business associates and used the time to learn to paint. Once she mastered the talent, she became one of the most respected artists in the area. Lottie died on November 7, 1899, after being accidentally poisoned by a druggist.

In between the times the local newspaper reported on the departed moving to the cemetery, it ran stories about the grave-yard's feuding caretakers. In the winter of 1879, the gravedigger and the town undertaker battled it out in court over the cost of their services. According to the *Bodie Daily Free Press,* "an interesting case" involving Pat Brown, the gravedigger, and H. Ward, the undertaker, passed before the local courts on December 9. "From the testimony it appears that Brown has dug 30 graves, and charged $162 for the work," the newspaper explained. "Twenty-five of these graves were occupied—the balance remaining tenant-less. Brown claimed that all he received was $17. The question arose as to whether he should receive pay for the uninhabited grave he had dug." A judge found in favor of Pat Brown and ordered that he be paid an additional $123 for the job he had done.

On December 21, 1879, Brown took Ward to court again to force him to pay for further services rendered. According to the *Bodie Daily Free Press,* "during the trial it came out that it cost more to bury a rich man than a poor man." The comment caused merriment among the spectators. It was explained that a rich man's coffin was placed in a big box, but a poor man was buried in a box just the size of the body."

The jury returned a verdict for Brown, and Ward was ordered to pay the gravedigger the sum of $124.

Death was a recurring part of time spent in the West and especially in Bodie. It was such a dominant presence in "Shooter's Town" that, with few exceptions, it inspired little notice. When President James A. Garfield was killed on September 19, 1881, no one could overlook his passing. Businesses draped their storefronts with black bunting and funeral services were held. Following a graveside ceremony in which an empty coffin carried by twelve pallbearers was placed in the ground, a procession of civic groups, miners, and Civil War veterans paraded behind a hearse drawn by six coal-black horses. Thousands of sad and reverent citizens stood in silence as mourners filed past.

In spite of the sobering truth that death was sure for all, some Bodie inhabitants possessed a sense of humor on the subject. Such frivolity was displayed in an article that ran in the December 3, 1879, edition of the *Bodie Daily Free Press.* It read, "KEEP THE GATE CLOSED! Someone left the gate of the cemetery open last night and let in a terrible draft of cold air. It was so cold that Bill Bodey got up and shut the gate with such a slam that both hinges were broken off. The residents of that section state that his language, on the occasion, was frightful."

The silent city that is the Bodie Odd Fellows Cemetery sits on a hill overlooking the sprawling town it was named after. Bodie became a state park in 1964 and is currently in an arrested state of decay. Thousands visit the site year-round and spend time walking through the graveyard inspecting the remnants of old wooden headboards that will eventually rot away.

Rattlesnake Dick

d. 1859

"Rattlesnake Dick dies; but never surrenders . . . "
— THE NOTE FOUND IN DICK BARTER'S HAND
WHEN HIS BODY WAS RECOVERED, 1859

It was the harsh treatment miner Dick Barter received from his fellow forty-niners that drove him outside the law. The notorious self-proclaimed "Pirate of the Placers" had tried unsuccessfully to live out his days as an honest citizen, but bad luck and his unfortunate capacity for making enemies made that way of life impossible.

By 1856 Barter had twice been in trouble over a matter of theft. Both times his innocence was proved, and he was released from custody. His reputation was ruined after that, however. He moved from Rattlesnake Bar in Placer County, California, to another mining camp in Shasta County and changed his name to Dick Woods. He was eventually recognized by a Bar resident passing through the area. Rumors about Barter being a thief caught up with him in his new home, and his bad luck started all over again.

This time Barter told an acquaintance, "I can't stand it any longer! I have been driven to it. Hereafter, my hand is against everyone and I suppose everyone is against me!" Barter decided that if he were to "have the name he might as well have the game too."

One night he poked his pistol into the face of a lonely traveler and got enough money to further his adventures in Northern California. Still young enough to require a seasoning of melodrama with his misdeeds, he told the victim that if anyone asked who robbed him to tell them it was Rattlesnake Dick.

"Rattlesnake Dick" Barter was described as naturally able and clever but selfish, vain, and devoid of the ordinary sense of right and wrong. He was one of those men whose course in life was governed by conditions that shaped his actions. One of those conditions was his debonair good looks and high enthusiasm. This irritated the men around him who were soured by ill fortune. ——

Rattlesnake Dick soon enlisted a group of six men to help him with his wholesale banditry and theft throughout the foothills of the Gold Country. The men robbed stores, cabins, stages, and gold shipments. Once honesty had been the rule throughout the canyons and gulches, a man could leave his tools and even his gold unguarded on his claim or in his cabin and no one thought of disturbing them. Now with Dick Barter and his gang on the loose, a new lawlessness sprang up throughout the area.

Rattlesnake Dick's career came to a bloody end on July 11, 1859. But just who fired the shot that killed the outlaw remains a mystery. Barter and his gang of highwaymen were all set to rob a stage full of gold when the sheriff and his deputies got the news of their whereabouts. Three deputies rode out to meet the bandits and were immediately engaged in a gunfight that left one deputy dead and another wounded. The deputy left standing insisted he had shot Rattlesnake Dick. He reported seeing him sway and come near to falling off his horse. The deputy was astonished to see the bandit rise in his saddle again and spur his horse down the road.

The next morning the body of Rattlesnake Dick was found lying in the road, a mile out of Auburn, California. His horse was nowhere to be found. Barter had been shot twice, both bullets

*Rattlesnake Dick, the "Pirate of the Placers,"
is buried in Auburn, California.*

PHOTOGRAPH BY CYNTHIA MARTIN

passed from his breast to his back. There was also a third bullet through the brain.

Newspaper accounts at the time speculate that Rattlesnake Dick must have realized he was too badly wounded to live. They believed he shot himself or ordered his companion to do it.

One month after Dick Barter was buried, an obscure item appeared in the local paper: "The horse of highwayman Rattlesnake Dick was found near Grass Valley, alive but with a bullet in the neck."

Historians record that this evidence pointed to the most tantalizing mystery in the whole story of Rattlesnake Dick. On that fatal July night, two of the deputies fired one shot each. The other deputy had no time to shoot. When Dick's body was found, there were two wounds in the breast and one through the head, the last supposedly his own or his companion's mercy shot. But whose bullet wounded the horse?

Rattlesnake Dick was laid to rest at the county's expense in the Old Auburn District Cemetery in Auburn in 1859. The outlaw's remains were moved when the town's new cemetery was founded in 1893. The tombstone over Barter's grave includes a common verse used on many headboards in the Old West: NO FURTHER SEEK HIS MERITS TO DISCLOSE, NOR DRAW HIS FRAILTIES FROM THEIR DREAD ADOBE. THEY THERE ALIKE IN TREMBLING HOPE REPOSE, THE BOSOM OF HIS FATHER AND HIS GOD.

Children of the Trail

ca. 1850s

Crude rock markers and wooden crosses dot the various trails used by settlers heading west in the mid-1800s. A significant number of those markers indicate the final resting places of children. The trek across the frontier was filled with peril. Violence, disease, and accidents claimed the lives of thousands of infants and toddlers. So uncertain were some pioneers of the longevity of their offspring born en route, they held off naming their babies until they were two years old.

The leading causes of death for children younger than age six traveling overland were cholera, meningitis, and smallpox. A number of children suffered fatal injuries when they fell under wagon wheels, fell into campfires, fell down steep canyons, or drowned in river crossings.

In 1852 a family from Kentucky who were caught up in the gold rush barely made it out of Independence, Missouri, when their four-year-old daughter died from meningitis. The leaders of the wagon train they were a part of stopped the caravan, and the men in the party cut down a medium-size oak tree to use as a casket for the girl. As carefully as possible they cut a slab off one side and hollowed the tree trunk. The girl's body was laid in the shell, and the slab was placed over it and nailed down. They dug a grave alongside the trail, lowered the impoverished casket, read a few words from the Bible, and prayed over the plot. After the grave was

PHOTOGRAPH BY CYNTHIA MARTIN

Flowers adorn a grave site in Nevada City, California, where six infants were buried in 1855. The marker simply reads: SIX BABIES.

filled in, they flattened it by driving the wagons back and forth over the fresh earth. Pioneers believed this action kept wild animals from digging up the area. When the trip resumed the mother of the deceased child stood in the rear of the wagon, staring back at the spot where they had left her daughter. She continued staring at the spot hours after the grave was out of sight.

An emigrant mother who lost her four-month-old child on the way to the fertile land of Oregon recorded a bit of the heart-breaking ordeal in her journal. In April 1852 Suzanna Townsend wrote, "we did feel very happy with her all the time she was with us and it was hard to part with her."

The journey across the rugged plains was so treacherous and risky some political leaders suggested only men should make the trip. In 1843 Horace Greeley wrote, "It is palpable homicide to tempt or send women and children over the thousand miles of precipice and volcanic sterility to Oregon."

Centuries-old cemeteries throughout the West are filled with small burial sites. More than one-third of the graves in the historic St. Patrick's Cemetery in Grass Valley, California, represent children who have long since been gone. As in many gold-mining-camp cemeteries, marble cherubs are the most common overseers of the graves. Sculptured lambs representing innocence were also frequently used.

The stories of the many lives that ended before they had a chance to make their mark on the frontier are lost forever. Only by their weathered tombstones are we able to know the tale of sacrifice to settle a new land.

Lola Montez

d. 1861

"Notorious I have always been and never famous."
— LOLA MONTEZ, 1854

In the mid-1850s gold rush prospectors filled theaters across the Old West to watch the vivacious entertainer Lola Montez perform the risqué spider dance. The provocative jig featured the shapely Lola dressed in a colorful, above-the-knee skirt, a corsetstyle blouse, and flesh-colored tights. Thousands of black corks, which represented spiders, dangled above her in the center of the stage. When the music began Lola would twirl around and wind herself up in the low-hanging props. Her flouncy skirt drifted to her thigh as she danced about trying to free herself from the man-made insects. The spectacular display brought audiences to their feet, cheering and begging for more, and Montez never denied her fans.

Although she presented herself to be of Latin decent, Lola was in fact from Ireland. She was born in 1818 and given the name Marie Dolores Eliza Rosanna Gilbert. She grew up to be a captivating beauty with dark, curly hair and black eyes. When she was still very young, Marie's parents arranged a marriage between their daughter and a sixty-year-old judge. Rather than settle down with a man so many years older than she was, Lola ran away from home and vowed to see the world. Not long after leaving her parents, she met and married a lieutenant in the British army. When he left her for another woman, Lola traveled to Madrid and began studying dance.

Her debut as a professional dancer was in London in 1847. She was billed as "The Premier Spanish Ballerina." In order to make the act seem more authentic, she changed her name to Lola Montez, adopted a Spanish accent, and claimed to be a Spaniard. Audiences adored her. She toured Europe, performing at all its royal courts, and she collected many male admirers along the way. Composer Franz Liszt, author Alexander Dumas, and Ludwig I, the king of Bavaria, were among her most famous lovers. By the time Lola Montez arrived in America, her reputation as a dancer and philanderer had preceded her. Theaters in New York, Boston, Philadelphia, and San Francisco were packed with curious citizens hoping to get a glimpse of the tempestuous entertainer.

Lured by the idea of becoming rich, Lola arrived in California in 1851. She had heard that miners readily tossed gold at the feet of performers and believed her singing and dancing act would separate the entertainment-starved men from a substantial portion of their wealth.

While performing in California's Gold Country, she met and married the owner of a newspaper, Patrick Hull. Her second marriage didn't fair any better than the first however, and the two divorced. An editor of a Grass Valley, California, newspaper criticized Lola for her failed marriages and what he called "an over all lack of morals." She was deeply offended by his comments and set out to confront the bold man. When she found him she threatened to beat him with her whip unless he apologized.

Lola Montez left California and the United States in 1855. From America she took her spider dance to Australia. Authorities there however banned the routine, calling it "immoral." With the

Lola Montez, 1821–1861

costly failure of the Australian tour, Lola returned to America to possibly recoup her losses. It was not to be, however. Lola's time had come and gone. She retired from the stage in 1858.

In 1859 she once again returned to New York, changed her name to Mrs. Fanny Gibbons, and began earning her living giving

The epitaph on the gravestone for Lola Montez at the Greenwood Cemetery in Brooklyn simply reads MRS. ELIZA GILBERT.

COURTESY OF THE GREENWOOD HISTORIC FUND

how-to-keep-your-beauty lectures. A year later she suffered a stroke and was left unable to speak.

News of her identity and pitiful condition hit the newspapers. The stories brought an old acquaintance to see her. Mrs. Isaac Buchanan promised to take care of her and moved her into the Buchanan home. Lola deeded all her possessions to the woman she saw as a benevolent friend. A few days after surrendering her worldly effects, the heartless rescuer installed her in a tenement bedroom in an area later known as Hell's Kitchen. Lola Montez died there in January 1861 at age forty-two. She left this world unrecognized and alone.

William Quantrill
d. 1865

"Kill! Kill! Lawrence must be cleansed and the only way to cleanse it is to kill! Kill!"
— WILLIAM QUANTRILL'S ORDER TO HIS SOLDIERS DURING A GUERRILLA RAID ON LAWRENCE, KANSAS, 1863

Dressed in his finest gray uniform and carrying four Colt revolvers tucked into a red sash tied around his waist, Captain William Clarke Quantrill paraded past a band of Rebel soldiers and grinned. The renegade bunch he led was 450 men strong. Among the brutal, ruthless fighters were such scoundrels as Frank and Jesse James and Cole and Jim Younger. Quantrill's unit had a reputation for being the most savage fighters in the Civil War. The captain and his command were more interested in robbery and murder than states' rights, however.

Quantrill was born in Canal Dover, Ohio, in 1837. Outside of the fact that he was an educated man who later became a schoolteacher, little is known about his youth. In 1858 he headed west to Utah and for a time made his living there as a gambler. An altercation with the law drove him back to the Midwest.

He began his military career in 1860 fighting for the North. He learned brutal guerrilla tactics from James H. Lane, commander of the Jayhawkers. The Jayhawkers was a nickname given to the antislavery men with the 7th Kansas Cavalry. Lane led a faction of extreme soldiers who burned and plundered towns sympathetic to the southern course. Quantrill was a Jayhawker at one time.

Quantrill eventually switched sides and became a Bushwacker, the equivalent of a Jayhawker for the South. After helping to capture Independence, Missouri, for the South in 1861, he quickly rose to the rank of captain and employed the same barbaric methods of battle Lane possessed. He assembled a fierce group of recruits willing to ransack property and gun down Northern supporters. The men, known as "Quantrill's Irregulars," staged numerous bloody raids. Their reputation grew and soon the Union army declared Quantrill and his raiders to be outlaws.

The highlight of Quantrill's merciless career happened on August 21, 1863, with a promise to cleanse entire towns of any and all "Yankee lovers." Captain Quantrill led the men into Lawrence, Kansas, and proceeded to toss men and women out of their homes into the street. The raiders then set fire to most of the buildings. While Lawrence burned, Quantrill had breakfast and ordered 150 men and boys to be rounded up and killed.

Union troops retaliated against Quantrill and chased the Irregulars out of the Midwest and into Texas. From there his men divided into two groups. Quantrill headed up one of those groups and gave command of the second to a vicious lieutenant named "Bloody" Bill Anderson.

Quantrill's time in Texas was short. He was quickly captured and arrested for murder by Union general McCulloch. Not long after being apprehended, he managed to escape and regroup with some of his troops. He then devised a plot to lead a small party of men to Washington, D.C., to assassinate Abraham Lincoln. The plan was thwarted in Lafayette County, Missouri, when Quantrill

William Quantrill was the leader of the most savage fighting unit in the Civil War.

recognized the superior Union force they were up against. He then fled to Kentucky, where he was shot in an ambush by Federal troops. The bullet, which lodged in his spine, was a fatal wound. Quantrill died at a military prison on June 6, 1865.

Some historians maintain that Quantrill was the most notorious and dangerous man in America's history. Many of the highly trained soldiers that served under Quantrill, such as Cole and Jim Younger and the James Brothers, employed his hit-and-run tactics when killing and looting. His criminal methods were also adopted by renegades in the Wild West, and desperados such as Frank Wolcott and Bob Rogers helped perpetuate his legacy of bloodshed on a new frontier.

Quantrill was buried in the Confederate Cemetery in Higginsville, Missouri. The small stone over his grave contains his name, the year he was born, and the year he died.

Julia Bulette

d. 1867

"She may be scarlet, but her heart is pure white."
— A VIRGINIA CITY MINER'S COMMENTS ABOUT
SOILED DOVE JULIA BULETTE, JULY 1861

Red, white, and blue bunting hung from the windows and awnings lining the main street of Virginia City, Nevada, on July 4, 1861. The entire mining community had turned out to celebrate the country's independence and share in the holiday festivities. The firemen of Fire Engine Company Number 1 led a grand parade through town. Riding on top of the vehicle and adorned in a fireman's hat and carrying a brass fire trumpet filled with roses was Julia Bulette.

The crowd cheered for the woman who had been named Queen of the Independence Day parade, and Julia proudly waved to them as she passed by. In that moment residents looked past the fact that she was a known prostitute who operated a busy parlor house. For that moment they focused solely on the charitable works she had done for the community and, in particular, the monetary contributions she had made to the fire department.

Julia Bulette had been born in London, England, in 1833. She and her family moved to New Orleans in 1848 and then on to California with the gold rush. Julia arrived in Virginia City in 1859

*Julia Bulette, known as the Queen of Sporting Row,
was murdered in 1867.*

after having survived a failed marriage and working as prostitute in Louisiana. In a western territory where the male inhabitants far out-numbered the female, doe-eyed Julia learned how to make that work to her advantage. She opened a house of ill repute and hired a hand-ful of girls to work for her.

Julia's Palace, as it came to be known, was a high-class estab-lishment complete with lace curtains, imported carpets, and velvet, high-back chairs. She served her guests the finest wines and French cooking and insisted that her gentlemen callers conduct themselves in a civilized fashion. She was noted for being a kind woman with a generous heart who never failed to help the sick and poor. In recog-nition of her support to the needy, the local firefighters made her an honorary member. It was a tribute she cherished and did her best to prove herself worthy of.

On January 21, 1867, Virginia City's beloved Julia was found brutally murdered in the bedroom of her home. The jewelry and furs she owned had been stolen. The heinous crime shocked the town, and citizens vowed to track the killer down.

The funeral provided for Julia was one of the largest ever held in the area. Businesses closed, and black wreaths were hung on the doors of the saloons. Members of the Fire Engine Company Number 1 pooled their money and purchased a silver-handled cas-ket for her burial. She was laid to rest at the Flowery Cemetery out-side Virginia City. The large wooden marker over her grave read simply JULIA.

Fifteen months after Julia's death, law enforcement appre-hended the man who robbed and killed her. Jean Millian had been one of her clients and had Julia's belongings on him when he was apprehended. Millian was tried, declared guilty, and hanged for the murder on April 27, 1868.

Flowery Cemetery is located east of Virginia City, Nevada, along Nevada Highway 341.

Kit Carson

d. 1868

"It's the prettiest country you've ever laid your eyes on. All we got to do is get over these mountains. Put your snowshoes on now and let's keep going."

— KIT CARSON'S WORDS TO A PARTY OF SETTLERS
HE LED THROUGH THE SIERRA NEVADAS, 1842

Stories about the acts of bravery the Indian agent, scout, and soldier Christopher "Kit" Carson performed were highly publicized in eastern newspapers in the 1850s and 1860s. Carson was recognized by the U.S. government as the best trailer in the West. His exploration of the Rocky Mountains gave way to clearer and safer paths to the new frontier.

He had been born in Kentucky on Christmas Eve in 1809. When he was one year old, his father moved the family to Howard County, Missouri, and purchased a homestead. Eight years later his father died fighting a fire that threatened to destroy the house and property. Kit Carson went to work to help support himself, his mother, and his siblings. He was an apprentice to a saddle maker, but the job he really longed for was that of trapper.

In 1824 he received an invitation from a seasoned frontiersman to travel to California. Carson eagerly accepted and earned his keep on the trek west by caring for the mules, horses, and oxen. Along the way the frontiersman took him under his wing and taught him all he needed to know to be a fur trapper.

For sixteen years Carson honed his skills as a trapper and led several fur expeditions through the Rockies along the Yellowstone, Bighorn, and Snake Rivers. During that time he became acquainted with many of the Native Americans living in the untamed territories. His first two wives were Apache Indians. His knowledge of the area and the relationship he had with the people who lived there made him a highly sought-after guide.

In 1842 army explorer John C. Fremont hired Carson to lead a patrol to Oregon and the Sacramento Valley in California. The trip was organized so that accurate maps of the terrain could be made. In their efforts to help settle the West, Carson and his team of explorers battled the elements and hostile Indians. Carson's heroism on the journey and as a soldier in the Mexican-American war earned him the rank of lieutenant in the United States Army.

When the war ended, Carson headed to Sante Fe and took up ranching with his third wife and four children. In 1853 the government appointed him the federal Indian agent for northern New Mexico. In 1862 he participated in the Civil War, organizing a volunteer infantry troop that saw action at Valverde. Carson retired from the army in 1866 and returned to work at his ranch. A year later he began suffering ill health and sought care from prominent physician H. R. Tilton. Tilton determined that his patient had an aneurysm and prescribed complete bed rest until it passed.

Carson spent his last days lying on the floor of the doctor's office on a buffalo robe. Despite the quality care he received, the aneurysm broke free and raced to his throat. His last words before he died on May 23, 1868, were, "Doctor, compadre . . . adios." Carson was fifty-nine years old. He was buried in Taos, New Mexico, alongside his third wife, who died a month after giving

Christopher Houston "Kit" Carson

Kit Carson was buried beside his third wife in 1868.

birth to a daughter. The cemetery was renamed the Kit Carson Cemetery after the legendary figure's death.

Carson was given a general's funeral, which was attended by hundreds of mourners, including H. R. Tilton; the assistant surgeon to the U.S. Army; and the Superintendent of Indian Affairs, Colonel Edward W. Wynkoop. Carson willed his property, valued at $7,000, to his children. The headstone that currently stands over his grave was erected by the Masons organization in 1908.

Wild Bill Hickok

d. 1876

*"I'd be willing to take an oath on the Bible that I have
killed over a hundred men."*

— WILLIAM BUTLER HICKOK TO REPORTER
H. M. STANLEY, FEBRUARY 1866

James Butler Hickok was known throughout the West as the
Prince of the Pistoleers. He had a serious disposition and fast gun
to back up any fight rogue cowhands challenged him to. His
exploits as a lawmen and talent with firearms made him a legend.

He was born on May 27, 1837, in Homer, Illinois. He had
five siblings, and his father was a farmer and owner-operator of a
general store. Hickok, who would grow to be more than six feet
tall, towered over the other boys in town and had a temper to
match his size. While still in his teens, he was involved in a violent
brawl with a freight-wagon driver. Fearing he might have killed the
man, Hickok left the area and headed west. His height, the way he
handled a gun, and the way he carried himself led to him being
offered a job as peace officer in Johnson County, Kansas. Hickok
took the position but only for a short time before hiring on with
Russell Majors and Waddell Freight Line as a teamster.

In the spring of 1860, Hickok was attacked by a bear while

on a wagon run through the Raton Pass. He killed the bear using a knife and two guns. After recuperating from his injuries, he moved to Nebraska, and the freight company he was working for assigned him to tend to the cattle and horses at a stage stop.

Hickok soon became embroiled in another scrape. He had been spending time with another man's mistress, and the man threatened to kill him. Hickok shot the scorned husband dead before his opponent's gun cleared his holster.

Following the incident in Nebraska, Hickok was again on the move. His travels took him to Sedalia, Missouri. From there he was employed as a "special detective" for the government. His job was to locate missing property such as weapons, ammunition, and other supplies that had been hijacked. The Civil War broke out during that time, and he signed on to help. Hickok used his skill as a sharpshooter to advance the cause of the Union army. He earned the handle "Wild Bill" fighting alongside General Samuel R. Curtis in the battle of Pea Ridge in Arkansas. For the bulk of the war, Hickok worked as a scout and wagon master for the North. He continued on in that role four years after the conflict between the states had ended, aiding cavalry troops in their quest to establish military posts in the West.

In between doing his duty for the country, Hickok was engaged in several bloody confrontations, killing every ambitious gunslinger who dared to take him on. News of his exploits preceded him wherever he traveled.

By the summer of 1869, Hickok had become the sheriff of Ellis County in Hays City, Kansas. He cleaned up the rowdy cow town, arresting drunken and disorderly military men, bank robbers, highwaymen, and horse thieves. Other rough settlements in the territory sent for Hickok to help them establish order as well. He became marshal of Abilene in March of 1871, and he crossed paths with such tough outlaws as John Wesley Hardin and Ben

*Wild Bill Hickok was shot in the
back of the head by Jack McCall in 1876.*

Thompson and gunman Phil Coe. Hickok was a respected lawman who went to great lengths to see that the rules of polite society were upheld.

He departed from the high profile role of law enforcement in 1872 and joined Buffalo Bill Cody's Wild West show. He traveled throughout the United States acting out stories from his rugged past and occasionally portraying George Armstrong Custer. After two years, he abandoned the stage and went west to Wyoming, stopping long enough to get married and then follow the gold strike to the Dakota Territory. Deadwood would be his last adventure.

James Butler "Wild Bill" Hickok

DEADWOOD, SOUTH DAKOTA, HISTORICAL SOCIETY

On August 2, 1876, Wild Bill Hickok bought in to a poker game at the No. 10 Saloon. He was seated with his back to the door, an uncomfortable position, but he could not persuade the gambler opposite him to trade seats. Later in the afternoon Jack McCall, a card player Hickok had won $10 off of the day before, entered the bar. He swore revenge on Wild Bill for taking his money and was ready to act on his threat. At twenty minutes after four, McCall walked up behind Hickok and shot him once in the head with a six-gun. Hickok fell sideways, toppled off his chair, and died as he hit the floor. The cards he continued to clutch to his hands were aces and eights—now referred to as the "Deadman's Hand."

Wild Bill Hickok's friend Charlie Utter claimed the famed lawman's body and placed the notice of his death in the *Black Hills Pioneer* newspaper. The notice read: "Died in Deadwood, Black Hills, August 2, 1876, from the effects of a pistol shot, J. B. Hickok (Wild Bill) formerly of Cheyenne, Wyoming. Funeral services will be held at Charlie Utter's Camp, on Thursday afternoon, August 3, 1876, at 3 o'clock, p.m. All are respectfully invited to attend."

Wild Bill Hickok was laid to rest with his Sharp's rifle, at Mount Moriah Cemetery in Deadwood. Almost the entire town attended the funeral. Utter had Hickok buried with a wooden grave marker that read WILD BILL HICKOK KILLED BY THE ASSASSIN JACK MCCALL IN DEADWOOD, BLACK HILLS, AUGUST 2ND, 1876. PARD, WE WILL MEET AGAIN IN THE HAPPY HUNTING GROUND TO PART NO MORE. GOODBYE, COLORADO CHARLIE C. H. UTTER.

In 1879, at the urging of Calamity Jane, Utter had Hickok's plot enclosed with cast-iron fence. The wooden grave marker over his burial site has since then been replaced by a stone bust of Wild Bill. Thousands visit the grave every year.

In accordance with her dying wish, Calamity Jane was buried next to Hickok.

Jack McCall was arrested, charged with murder, and later hanged.

Little Bighorn Cemetery

1876

*"As Lt. James Bradley rode over a rise, he spied a large
number of white objects, which turned out to be dead
cavalrymen. He rode hurriedly over the field, and in a
few minutes time counted one hundred and ninety-seven
bodies."*

— A BRIEF ACCOUNT FROM A SCOUTING PARTY
THAT FOUND GENERAL GEORGE ARMSTRONG
CUSTER AND HIS ARMY (*HELENA HERALD*,
MONTANA, JULY 15, 1876)

A raw wind blew snow flurries past the face of a well-dressed elderly lady studying the tombstones that filled the Custer Battlefield
National Cemetery. Elizabeth, General George A. Custer's widow,
stared down at the numerous graves, only the wind could be
heard. The distinguished seventy-year-old woman was alone at the
location, remembering the day she was informed that her famous
husband had perished at the Battle of Little Bighorn.

On May 17, 1876, Elizabeth had kissed George good-bye and
wished him good fortune in his efforts to fulfill the army's orders to
drive in the Native Americans who would not willingly relocate to a
reservation. Adorned in a black taffeta dress and a velvet riding cap
with a red peacock feather that matched George's red scarf, she

watched the proud regiment ride off. It had been a splendid picture.

Flags and pennons were flying, men were waving, and even the horses seemed to be arching themselves to show how fine and fit they were. George rode to the top of a promontory and turned around, stood up in his stirrups, and waved his hat. After a moment he and his men started forward again and in a few seconds disappeared; horses, flags, men, and ammunition—all on their way to the Little Bighorn River. That was the last time Elizabeth saw her husband alive.

Confirmation of Custer's death and that of his entire regiment reached Elizabeth on June 26, 1876. Captain William S. McCaskey, a courier sent to deliver the devastating news, held his hat in his hand as he addressed the general's wife. Elizabeth stared at the officer, her eyes pleading. "None wounded, none missing, all dead," he sadly reported. She stood frozen for a moment, unable to move, the color drained from her face.

"I'm sorry, Mrs. Custer," the captain sighed. "Do you need to sit down?"

Elizabeth blinked away the tears. "No," she replied. "What about the other wives?"

"We'll let them know of their husbands' fates," he assured her.

"I'm coming with you," she said, choking back more tears. "As the wife of the post commander, it's my duty to go along with you when you tell the other . . . widows." The captain didn't argue with the bereaved woman.

In the early spring of 1912, Elizabeth made a pilgrimage to the graveyard to pay homage to the fallen men in her late husband's command. The battlefield was designated a national cemetery in 1879. Thousands of tourists have visited the site, which pays tribute not only to the westward advance of the American frontier but also to the last phases of the Indian's struggle to hold onto their lands and way of life.

*The Little Bighorn National Battlefield was preserved
as a cemetery in 1879.*

White marble markers stand over the various spots where the
265 soldiers fell and were initially buried. In 1881 the majority of
the remains of the troops were exhumed and moved to a central
location surrounding a granite monument.

Among the men who died at the Little Bighorn were three
of Custer's relatives. His brothers Tom and Boston and his
nephew, Harry, all fell in the fight. Harry Armstrong, also known
as Autie Reed, and Boston Custer were civilians working with the
7th Cavalry. Boston was a quartermaster employee assigned to the
pack train accompanying the troops. The bodies of Tom, Boston,
and Harry were mutilated by the Indians they fought. Tom's
body was disfigured almost beyond recognition. Out of respect
for the celebrated "Yellow-haired General," George's remains
were left intact.

Other notable tombstones are that of Scout Isaiah Dorman,
the only African American in the battle, and Private Frank Braun,
who was the last to die from injuries sustained during the fighting.

Mitch Bouyer, a 7th Cavalry scout and interpreter who was half Sioux, perished at the Little Bighorn, as did Private Alexander Stella, the only soldier in the regiment from Greece.

A few grave markers list the names of men who joined the army using a false handle. For reasons that have never been revealed, Private John Dolan enlisted as Thomas Brown and Private George W. Glease enlisted as George W. Glenn. Both men were killed and stripped of their possessions. Many of the soldiers who were slain during the battle were robbed of their personal items and clothing. Army surgeon Holmes O. Paulding noted in his journal the "deprived condition" in which he found the troops when he inspected the carnage on June 26, 1876. He happened onto the clothing of two officers whose remains were never found. "I picked up a buckskin shirt from which the skin had been stripped and marked with the name Porter," Paulding wrote. "Poor fellow, there was a hole under the right shoulder and blood over the rest."

Several of the regiments lie side by side at the cemetery. Privates George Horn, John Burkham, and Archibald McIlhargey rest near the grave of Corporal Henry Scollin. Scollin shared a premonition of his pending death with a Private Daniel Newell from a separate regiment. "In less than 24 hours," Newell reported to his superiors, "Henry was lying dead on the bottom of Little Big Horn, his body riddled with bullets."

The granite monument that looms over the markers at the cemetery bears the name of all the officers and soldiers killed in battle. A separate tombstone commemorates the cavalry horse that died on the spot and includes the remains of thirty-nine mounts that carried troops into battle.

Custer Battlefield National Cemetery was originally established as a final resting place for the 7th Cavalry, but it was later expanded to include deceased veterans of all wars and their dependents. The memorial park contains more than five thousand graves. It was officially closed to any further burials in 1977.

Although there are tombstones with George Custer's name and his brother's etched across them, the brothers' bodies were moved to different locations. Elizabeth had General Custer buried at West Point in New York, and Captain Thomas Custer is buried at the Fort Leavenworth National Cemetery in Kansas.

Tombstone's Boot Hill

Founded 1878

"We never did hang the wrong one but once or twice, and them fellers needed to be hung anyhow jes' on general principles."

—A NAMELESS JUDGE IN THE OLD WEST

The remains of some of Tombstone's most famous and infamous rest in peace at historic Boot Hill graveyard. From 1878 to 1884, pioneers, Indian scouts, outlaws, crime victims, civic leaders, and town founders were buried there.

Tombstone, the notorious Old West locale, came into being in 1877. Miner Ed Schieffen discovered silver in the southwest corner of the state and named his find the Tombstone. News of the rich strike spread, and an avalanche of settlers converged on the area. By late 1881, more than seven thousand people lived in or around the Arizona boomtown. In addition to the hopeful prospectors and their families came the lawless, violent types. They frequented the gambling houses, taverns, and brothels that lined the thoroughfare.

The gun-toting outlaws shot their way in and out of such well-known stops as the Bird Cage Theatre, Crystal Palace, and Oriental Saloon. The criminal behavior became so out of control in Tombstone that in 1880 President Chester A. Arthur declared martial law and sent in troops from nearby army post Fort Huachuca to bring about order.

Sinners who met their demise in drunken brawls, jealous rages, and crooked poker games were taken to a lot of land on the side of a hill overlooking the northern portion of town. The sagebrush-covered field acquired the name Boot Hill because it was filled with people who had died suddenly—with their boots on.

Most of the bodies buried at Boot Hill could be identified, and the wooden or stone headboards that mark the graves list their names. Some remains, however, lie on the hill under the inscription UNKNOWN. One such grave contains the body of a man found in 1882 at the abandoned Minute Mine at the bottom of a sixty-foot shaft. According to the tombstone, HE WAS WELL-DRESSED, INDICATING THAT HE WAS NOT A MINER.

A number of graves belong to thieves, cardsharps, murderers, and rustlers. Some of the names on the tombstones were recognized scoundrels and outlaws. Charley Storms was a professional gambler shot by gunfighter Luke Short. Short had killed so many men he was given the nickname the "undertaker's friend." Storms's grave marker includes his name and the year he was gunned down: 1882. It also reads GUNS BLAZED AGAIN AS THESE TWO GAMBLING MEN MET. STORMS WAS SHOT IN FRONT OF THE ORIENTAL SALOON, WHERE SHORT DEALT CARDS.

Lester Moore's headboard became popular not so much because of the man but because of the verse inscribed under his handle. HERE LIES LESTER MOORE, FOUR SLUGS FROM A .44. NO LESS, NO MORE. Moore was a Wells Fargo agent who was shot over a dispute about a delivery.

Tombstone's Boot Hill is the place of interment for several criminals who were hanged for a variety of misdeeds. An angry mob strung up John Heath on February 22, 1884. Ironically, the lynching took place a short distance from the county courthouse. His marker simply carries his name.

Dan Dowd, Red Sample, Tex Howard, Bill Delaney, and Dan Kelley were all legally hanged on March 8, 1884. The host of bandits was found guilty of murder and robbery. Their mutual grave is marked by a weathered piece of wood bearing only their names.

The remains of numerous gunfight victims are scattered throughout the cemetery. Among them are men who fell at the gunfight at the OK Corral. They aren't the only ones to meet their maker by way of a six-gun, but they are the most famous.

Among others who died by the gun was Chas Helm, a local rancher. A neighboring rancher killed him in 1882 after a quarrel over how to drive cattle. William Clayborne shot James Hickey in the head in 1882 after demanding the man join him in a drink. Dick Toby was gunned down by Sheriff Behan in 1881. The wooden markers of all these men contain their names and year of death.

Tombstone's Chinatown is represented in the Boot Hill Cemetery by such names as Quong Kee and Hop Lung. Kee owned and operated a restaurant and was initially buried in a pauper's plot. His body was later moved by the townspeople who knew and respected him. No information exists about the life and death of Hop Lung. Both men died in 1880.

A pair of soiled doves keep company with the predominately male residents of the graveyard. Dutch Annie, also known as the Queen of the Red Light District, was the proverbial prostitute with a heart of gold who helped out anyone in need. More than a thousand mourners attended her graveside service. Annie's tombstone and the tombstone of a woman known as Margarita have crosses over their graves with their names on them.

Margarita's life ended at the hands of a fallen woman named Little Gertie. The two fought over cowboy Billy Milgreen (known as Gold Dollar) at a dance. Little Gertie had been Gold Dollar's woman until the dark-eyed beauty Margarita persuaded him to spend time with her. Gertie caught up with the temptress and the two argued. She then stabbed Margarita in the stomach with a jagged knife.

When a new Tombstone Cemetery was established in 1884, the Boot Hill graveyard fell into disrepair. Left neglected for more than fifty years, the land overtook the graves, and souvenir hunters stole what the elements did not destroy. A restoration effort was put into effect in 1940. The plots were cleaned up and new markers put into place.

Included in the restoration was an area designated for those pioneers of Jewish decent, whose graves were once surrounded by an eight-foot-high wall. During the more than a century it has been standing, the adobe-brick structure has eroded away to a mere four feet.

Ten states across the United States have at least one cemetery called Boot Hill. Tombstone, Arizona's Boot Hill, is easily one of the most renowned graveyards in the Wild West.

Charley Parkhurst

d. 1879

*"The most dexterous and celebrated of the California
drivers, and it was an honor to occupy the spare end of
the driver's seat when the fearless Charley Parkhurst held
the reins."*

— A TEAMSTER'S COMMENTS TO THE
SAN FRANCISCO MORNING CALL, 1879

When Charley Parkhurst, the famed stagecoach driver of the Sierra
Nevada foothills, died in December 1879, an interesting discovery
was made. The sixty-seven-year-old rough-talking, cigar-smoking
whip master was in fact a woman. The fifty-year masquerade began
as a way for the desperate Parkhurst to acquire work.

Parkhurst was born in Lebanon, New Hampshire, in 1812.
Her parents were poor and abandoned her shortly after naming
her Charlotte. The majority of Charlotte's early life was spent at an
orphanage. The facility was a particularly harsh environment, and
the children were treated cruelly. Charlotte ran away as soon as she
was old enough to attempt to make it on her own. She was fifteen
years old when she left the orphanage, and she disguised herself as
a boy to keep from being caught by the authorities.

On the outside she soon learned that there were many more

job opportunities for men than women. With that in mind she decided to keep up the charade of being a male, taking her efforts a bit further and changing her name to Charles.

Charles Parkhurst's first job was working at a stable in Worcester, Massachusetts. She performed a variety of duties involving the care and feeding of horses and mules. She fell in love with the animals and learned how to handle a team. In a short time she was an expert driver. Her talent as a coachman did not go unnoticed by competing stage businesses. She quickly became a highly sought-after whip master. In January 1850 she accepted a job from a pair of wealthy entrepreneurs who had started a gold rush transport company in California.

A flood of humanity had converged on the hills outside of Sacramento, and the need for a carriage business was great. Charley worked for the California line hauling miners from their claims to various points in between. Since she dressed in well-worn trousers, an old waistcoat, and shirt, and sported a large Texas hat, it was easy for passengers to be fooled about her gender. Her scarred facial features added to the illusion. A cantankerous horse had kicked her in the face when she was in her early twenties, and the incident left her disfigured and minus an eye. She wore a black patch over the injury. She was five feet, seven inches tall and had a low and raspy voice. Charley Parkhurst carried herself like a man, as well. The passengers she drove were impressed with the fearless way she handled robbers or hostile natives who tried to stop her coach. She outran or outshot anyone who attempted to hold up the ride.

Some of the crude paths Charley traveled were treacherous. They consisted of little more than a rocky strip of barren earth through low-hanging trees etched out in the sides of cliffs. She guided her team of horses over the narrow embankments with great confidence. Other whips boasted of her ability and maintained that

A drawing of famed stagecoach driver Charley Parkhurst leading her team through the foothills of California

she could run both wheels of her stage over a quarter lying in the road with her horses going at top speed.

Her arrival into the mining camps and big towns that dotted the West Coast was an impressive scene. Major A. N. Judd, a soldier who had ridden with Charley, wrote in his memoirs that "when she pulled into a stage stop with a beautifully equipped 20-passenger Concord coach . . . it was an inspiring sight indeed." Judd also described her skills as a driver and called her the "greatest whip in the west."

"Every move (she made) played its part." He continued, "One would note with what dexterity she plied the brakes just right in order to stop with the door just opposite the main entrance to the hotel."

In addition to Charley being a skilled driver, she was also a kind one. She frequently shared her earnings with those in need, assisted the sick, and set broken bones. At the end of her rides, she watered and fed the horses herself and even bunked with them. It was said of Charley Parkhurst that he was "a great friend to all manner of life."

In 1868 Charley registered to vote and in November of that year became the first woman to cast a ballot. The historic event was recognized eleven years later after Parkhurst had died.

If not for the coming of the railroad, Charley would have continued driving a stage for the rest of her life. The new mode of transportation forced her to retire in 1874. In her early sixties and living on her ranch in Santa Cruz, Charley struggled with rheumatism and cancer of the throat and mouth. She died of cancer on December 29, 1879. She was sixty-seven.

Charley's true gender was not realized until her body was being prepared by a physician for burial. The news that he was a she spread quickly among local residents, but the information about her true sex did not reach beyond the area for several days.

The initial response from newspapers across the country to Charley's demise was one of remorse and reverence, but after the news that Parkhurst had been masquerading as a man for many years, additional reference to the teamster was less compassionate. The press called her a "hermaphrodite." Editors at the *Rhode Island Gazette* were so outraged by the revelation they wrote a scathing article about her passing. "Charley Parkhurst died of a malignant disease," the article read. "She could act and talk like a man, but when it came to imitating a man's reticence, nature herself revolted, and the lifelong effort to keep from speaking, except when she had something to say, resulted at last in death from cancer of the tongue."

Some of Charley's friends were equally appalled when they learned the truth about her. One associate expressed concern over the gender of his other acquaintances. "I don't trust anyone anymore," he told a reporter for the *Yreka Union* newspaper.

A number of people who remembered Charley for the gracious, loyal person she was attended her funeral. There is no information as to whether or not her real gender was mentioned at the service. An article in the *San Francisco Chronicle* suggested that "it is useless to waste time in conjectures as to what led the dead to take up the cross of a man's laboring life."

Charley was laid to rest at the Pioneer Cemetery in Watsonville, Santa Cruz County, California. The tombstone reads CHARLEY DARKEY PARKHURST.

John Sutter
d. 1880

*"The country swarmed with lawless men. I was alone
and there was no law."*

— JOHN A. SUTTER, JUNE 1848

The life of Captain John Augustus Sutter, the German-Swiss pioneer, dramatically changed when gold was discovered on his property on January 24, 1848, and the West was transformed into a land teeming with eager prospectors. When Sutter emigrated from Switzerland hoping to make his fortune in America, he scarcely could have imagined the impact the glittering lumps of gold found near his sawmill in Coloma, California, would have on his future and that of the emerging nation.

Sutter was born February 15, 1803, in Kandern Baden, Germany, a few miles from the Swiss border. He received his formal education in the village of Neuchatel, Switzerland. At age thirteen he became an apprentice to a firm of printers and booksellers, and although he was a diligent worker, the trade did not suit him. He ventured into business, owning and operating a dry goods store. In addition to managing his store, he served as a lieutenant in the Swedish Army Reserve Corps.

John Augustus Sutter, 1803–1880

LIBRARY OF CONGRESS, LCUSZ62-133637

Due in part to his expensive way of living, Sutter eventually ran into trouble with his debtors and lost the store. In May 1834 he fled the area and his creditors and headed for America, leaving behind a wife and five children.

Shortly after arriving in New York, Sutter was able to reestablish himself in the business world. His spending habits had not changed, however, and he fell into the same desperate financial situation as before. Again he ran, and this time he ended up in St. Louis, Missouri, where he worked as an innkeeper and merchant.

Then four years after his arrival in the States, and with a goal of building an agricultural empire, he joined the American Fur Company and headed west.

After taking a brief detour to the Hawaiian Islands, Sutter made it to Monterey, California. He was driven to see his dream realized and met with the leader of the territory, Governor Alvarado, to discuss the possibility of establishing a business. As soon as the initial permission was granted, Sutter secured two schooners filled with supplies and sent them down the Sacramento River. Two weeks later the vessels landed at the location where the American River meets the Sacramento.

The native peoples around the area where Sutter had disembarked did not like the foreign control of their land. They harassed him because of his association with the government in power. But Sutter made treaties with the Indians and dealt fairly with them in all matters. He gained their trust and friendship, and later they actually worked for him.

By becoming an official Mexican citizen on August 29, 1840, Sutter successfully acquired a land grant. The following year he began construction on a fort that would become the headquarters for all newcomers to California. Miwok and Nisenam Indians, Mexicans, and Hawaiians were hired to work and guard the fort and the forty-eight acres of land surrounding the site. The fort housed a distillery, a flour mill, a bakery, and a blacksmith and carpentry shop. Several head of cattle and numerous horses grazed on the fields around the property, as well as sheep, chickens, and pigs. The fort grew to become a necessary stop for emigrants who traveled west.

In 1847 Sutter contracted to build a sawmill on the South Fork of the American River, fifty miles east of Sutter's Fort, with the carpenter and pioneer James Marshall. Marshall had the sawmill partially completed when he discovered gold while walking along the clear banks of the water.

The Swiss pioneer John Sutter became famous when gold was discovered on his land in 1848. He died a pauper in 1880.

At the time of the find that started the gold rush, Sutter's assets were at their height. After several years of growth, the fort was self-contained. But the gold find brought him harm, not fortune, as his land was suddenly overrun with squatters. They slaughtered his cattle at will and helped themselves to the rest of his livestock. His wheat fields were trampled, his lumber and gristmills were deserted and dismantled, and hides were left to rot in his tannery. His workers, even the Native Americans, abandoned him for the goldfields.

Broke and desperate, Sutter fled with his newly arrived family to a farm near Yuba City, California. By 1865, having seen his fort reduced to one building and his farm burned to the ground, Sutter moved to Lititz, Pennsylvania. He lived out the remainder of his days near poverty. From 1865 to 1880 Sutter lobbied Congress for compensation for the loss of land for which he had paid thousands of dollars in taxes. Year after year political leaders told him that the matter would be addressed and settled, but it was never fully resolved.

On June 20, 1880, John Sutter, California's oldest and most notable pioneer, died of heart failure. He was seventy-seven years old. His funeral was attended by several well-known individuals he had befriended during his extraordinary life, including General Phil Sheridan and Mark Twain.

Sutter's eulogy was delivered by Western Expedition leader General John Charles Fremont. Sutter was laid to rest in the Moravian Brotherhood's Cemetery in Lititz, Pennsylvania.

Billy the Kid

d. 1881

*"He was the only kid who ever worked here who never
stole anything."*

— BILLY THE KID'S EMPLOYER AT THE
SILVER CITY HOTEL IN NEW MEXICO

William H. Bonney, better known as Billy the Kid, drifted
through New Mexico in the mid-1870s, defying the law and
becoming famous in the process. By the time he turned age sixteen, he had killed one man and been jailed twice. Desperate circumstances and a misplaced sense of justice was what spurred
Billy on toward his life of crime.

Born in New York on November 23, 1859, Billy was the
younger of two boys. His father died in 1864, leaving Billy's mom
alone to look after the children. In 1873 she moved her sons to
Indiana, where she met and married a man named William Antrim.
Antrim took his new wife and her family to Silver City, New
Mexico. A gold and silver strike there made the town rich with
possibilities. The four no sooner arrived than William Antrim
abandoned his new family to prospect. Billy's mother managed a
hotel to support her boys, and Billy worked with her. In 1874 she
was diagnosed with tuberculosis and died shortly thereafter. Billy
was fourteen years old.

William H. Bonney, aka Billy the Kid, 1859–1881

Not long after his mother's death, Billy had his first run-in with the law. The clothes he stole from a Chinese launderer's business were meant to be a teenage prank, but the act was perceived as malicious theft to the local authorities. Wanting to teach Billy a lesson, the sheriff decided to lock him up. After spending two days in jail, Billy escaped and made his way to Arizona.

In 1877 Billy was hired on at a sawmill at the Camp Grant Army Post. The blacksmith who worked at the military post was a bully of sorts and took an instant dislike to Billy. He frequently made fun of him, taunting him until the teenager snapped and called the blacksmith a name. That was the cue he was waiting for and he attacked Billy, and Billy shot him. He was arrested for the killing the following day and subsequently escaped.

Billy roamed about New Mexico's Pecos Valley in Lincoln County, working odd jobs at various ranches and farms. Wealthy English cattle barren John Tunstall eventually offered the restless young man full-time employment to watch his livestock. Billy took on the job with great zeal—Tunstall was kind to him, and Billy appreciated his integrity.

Not everyone felt that way about Tunstall. A pair of rival merchants and livestock owners who were resentful of his riches were determined to destroy the man and his holdings. The heated battle, which erupted between the established business owners and ranchers who had a monopoly on beef contracts for the army, and entrepreneurs such as John Tunstall, was referred to as the Lincoln County War.

As an employee of John Tunstall's, William Bonney found himself in the middle of the feud. It became a personal battle for him when the disgruntled ranchers had Tunstall gunned down. Billy first joined in with law enforcement to help bring the murderers in legally, but he ended up being jailed for interfering with the sheriff and his deputies. After his release Billy decided to take

PALS

TOM
O'FOLLIARD
DIED DEC. 1880

WILLIAM H.
BONNEY
ALIAS
"BILLY THE KID"
DIED JULY 1881

CHARLIE BOWDRE
DIED DEC. 1880

PHOTOGRAPH BY CYNTHIA MARTIN

William H. Bonney was buried in Fort Sumner's Old Cemetery between
his friends Tom O'Folliard and Charlie Bowdre in July 1881.

matters into his own hands and joined a posse bent on hunting
down the killers. When the murderers were located, Billy and the
other members of the vendetta riders, known as the Regulators,
shot them dead.

The Lincoln County War ended in a fiery blaze on July 19,
1878, and a number of men were killed. Billy kept the Regulators
together, and the boys ventured into cattle rustling. More people
were killed along the way and Billy the Kid, as he was now called,
was a wanted man. So Billy negotiated a deal with the governor of
the state. If Billy turned himself in to the proper authorities and
gave them information about those who participated in the

Lincoln County War, he could go free. When the deal was agreed upon, Billy laid down his weapons and submitted to the arrest.

After Billy was incarcerated, the district attorney went against the governor's arrangement with the Kid and promised to see him hanged. An enraged Billy the Kid escaped from jail and went on the run—managing to elude the authorities for two years.

In 1880 Pat Garrett was sworn in as the new Lincoln County sheriff and assigned the duty of apprehending Billy the Kid. He had a reputation as a determined lawman and expert tracker, and he was persistent in his efforts to bring the Kid to justice. After laying several traps for Bonney, Garrett arrested him in April 1881. Billy the Kid was tried, found guilty, and sentenced to be hanged, but he escaped before making it to the gallows.

Garrett again pursued the young fugitive and caught up with him after two months. Billy the Kid was hiding at a ranch near Fort Sumner, New Mexico. Under the cover of darkness, Garret waited for Billy to appear and then shot him on sight. "All this occurred in a moment," Garrett later told journalists. "Quickly as possible I drew my revolver and fired, threw my body aside and fired again . . . the Kid fell dead. He never spoke," Garrett explained. "A struggle or two, a little strangling sound as he gasped for breath, and the Kid was with his many victims."

Garrett went on to describe the scene of the outlaw's demise as a sad occasion for those closest to him. "Within a very short time after the shooting, quite a number of native people had gathered around, some of them bewailing the death of a friend, while several women pleaded for permission to take charge of the body, which we allowed them to do. They carried it across the yard to a carpenter's shop, where it was laid out on a workbench, the women placing lighted candles around it according to their ideas of properly conducting a 'wake for the dead.'"

On July 16, 1881, the day after Billy the Kid was shot, he was buried at the Old Fort Sumner Cemetery (a military cemetery) in DeBaca County, New Mexico. He was placed in the same grave as his friends Tom O'Folliard and Charlie Bowdre. Both boys had been shot and killed by Garrett and his men in December 1880. The single tombstone standing over the plot lists the three desperados' names and the word PALS.

Over the years a handful of New Mexico residents have come forward with information that Garrett supposedly shared with them about the killing. They claimed the sheriff told them the Kid got away the night of the ambush and the man at the burial site was a fellow bandit.

A Texas man by the name of Ollie "Brushy Bill" Roberts of Hico, Texas, claimed he was the real Billy the Kid. He insisted he faked his death the night Garrett came looking for him and had been on the run ever since. Brushy Bill died in 1950.

Several attempts have been made to exhume the Kid's remains and that of his mother so DNA testing could be done and the controversy laid to rest. The courts have denied the requests, stating they were "unnecessary and unreasonable."

The Clantons and McLaurys

d. 1881

*"For my handling of the situation at Tombstone, I have
no regrets. Were it to be done again, I would do it exactly
as I did it at the time."*

— WYATT EARP'S COMMENTS ABOUT THE
GUNFIGHT AT THE OK CORRAL, 1901

The legend of the thirty second gunfight that took place outside
the OK Corral in Tombstone, Arizona, made the town and the
men involved famous. The feud between the Earp brothers, Doc
Holliday, the Clantons, and the McLaurys reached its dramatic
point on October 26, 1881. When the smoke cleared after the six-
shooters and shotguns were fired, three men lay dead in the street.

The so-called sinners in the deadly drama were Frank and
Tom McLaury and Billy Clanton. The Clantons and McLaurys
were ranchers who had stolen much of the livestock they owned.
Their thievery kept them in constant trouble with Tombstone's
law enforcement. When Wyatt, Morgan, and Virgil Earp arrived
on the scene and eventually became town sheriff and deputies,
respectively, they vowed to bring order to the territory. It was just
a matter of time before they would be forced to deal with the
notorious cowboy lawbreakers.

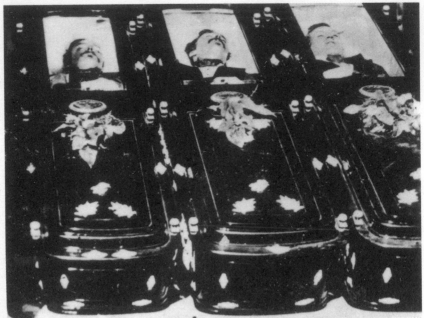

*Tom and Frank McLaury and Billy Clanton lie in state
after their deaths at the gunfight at the OK Corral.*

Wyatt Earp particularly disliked the Clantons and their less then legal dealings. The Clantons and McLaurys equally resented the Earps and Holliday for interfering in their business affairs. On the morning of October 26, news reached Wyatt that Ike Clanton and his cohorts were in Tombstone threatening to "shoot an Earp." The rustlers and lawmen spent most of the afternoon antagonizing one another verbally and physically. By two o'clock a street fight seemed inevitable.

The Earps and Holliday had heard that Ike and Billy Clanton and Tom and Frank McLaury were armed and waiting for them at the OK Corral. Virgil led the way to the cowboys with the intention of disarming the men. Wyatt, Virgil, Doc, and Morgan walked four abreast down the street. When they reached the stable, the Clanton gang was waiting for them. County Sheriff John Behan made a feeble attempt to stop the fight that was coming, but he was dismissed.

The men stood a mere six feet apart when the bullets started flying. Wyatt shot Frank McLaury in the stomach and killed him. Ike panicked and ran off. Billy Clanton was hit in the chest and wrist. Doc unloaded his weapon into Tom McLaury's right side. With the exception of Wyatt, the Earps and Doc sustained a few non-life-threatening injuries.

Two days after the gun battle, friends and sympathizers of the Clantons gathered on the main street of town to join the funeral procession for the McLaury boys and Billy Clanton. After their bodies had been laid out in silver-trimmed caskets, they were displayed in the window of the local hardware store and then transported to the cemetery in glass-sided hearses. A brass band followed a procession of mourners carrying signs that read "Murdered on the Streets of Tombstone."

Ike Clanton and his followers vowed revenge for the murders of Billy, Tom, and Frank. Two months after the gunfight at the OK Corral, Morgan Earp was gun downed while playing pool at a saloon on Allen Street. Virgil was permanently wounded by a buckshot blast that shattered his arm.

Wyatt gathered a posse of supporters and rode out to avenge his brother's killing. After shooting several cowboys who had sided with the Clantons and who had been involved in killing Morgan and injuring Virgil, Wyatt officially ended his vendetta tour.

Billy Clanton and Frank and Tom McLaury were buried at Tombstone's Boot Hill. Those who witnessed the gunfight at OK Corral reported that the dead men's last words were "gut-wrenching." Billy is reported to have said, "They have murdered me! I've been murdered." Tom McLaury said, "I have got

PHOTOGRAPH BY CYNTHIA MARTIN

Billy Clanton and Frank and Tom McLaury have three of the most
famous graves at Tombstone's Boot Hill Cemetery.

nothing." And just before being shot to death, Frank pointed his
gun at Doc Holliday and said, "I have you now."

Tombstone's Boot Hill is located on State Highway 80 in
Tombstone, Arizona.

Jesse James
d. 1882

"All the world likes an outlaw. For some damn reason they remember 'em."

—Jesse James, 1879

Many towns, cities, farms, and plantations from Missouri to Georgia were left in ruin at the conclusion of the Civil War in 1865. Confederate guerrilla soldiers, resentful of the Union's treatment of their families, property, and possessions, continued to lash out against them well after the battle between the states had ended.

Jesse James was the most notorious of all the rebels at that time. He and his brother Frank formed a gang of Southern sympathizers and set out to rob banks controlled by the North. The James gang's career began on February 13, 1866, when they staged their first holdup at the Commercial Bank of Liberty, Missouri.

Jesse James was born in Clay County, Missouri, on September 5, 1847. His father, Robert, was a Baptist preacher who died when Jesse was four years old. His mother, Zerelda, was a hard-working farm woman who ruled the home with an iron fist and sheltered her sons from criticism about their rebellious nature.

At the age of seventeen, Jesse followed in the footsteps of his

Jesse Woodson James, age seventeen

older brother, Frank, who was fighting in the Civil War. Jesse, Frank, and family friend Cole Younger were all part of William Clarke Quantrill's Raiders. Jesse's skills as a horseman and expert shot were further improved while serving under William "Bloody

Bill" Anderson. Anderson instigated a fiery raid on Lawrence, Kansas, in August 1863, and both Jesse and Frank were a part of the brutal ordeal.

Less than a year after the Civil War ended, Jesse James led ten men on what would be the first of many robberies. His reputation as the United States version of Robin Hood sprung from rumors that Jesse shared a portion of his ill-gotten gain with struggling Southerners. For more than fifteen years, Jesse James and his gang held up railroads and banks throughout the Midwest.

Jesse's last robbery occurred on August 7, 1881. Jesse and his gang, which at this time included Frank James, Wood and Clarence Hite, Dick Liddell, and Charlie and Bob Ford, stopped a train outside of Blue Cut, Missouri. The bandits busted open the safe on board, which reportedly had $15,000 inside. When the men found the safe contained a meager $1,500, they decided to rob the passengers to try to make up the difference.

On April 3, 1882, Jesse called the Ford brothers to his home in St. Joseph, Missouri, to discuss plans to rob the Platte County bank. It had been more than a year since Jesse and his gang had worked together. Unbeknownst to the legendary outlaw, Bob and Charlie Ford had negotiated a deal with Missouri governor Thomas Crittenden to kill Jesse. The reward offered for the deed was $10,000.

Jesse escorted the Fords into the parlor and began explaining the details of the job. When Jesse paused for a moment to straighten a picture frame hanging on the wall, Bob unloaded his pistol into the back of his head. According to the Ford brothers' account of the incident, Jesse turned to look the assailants in the face before he fell lifeless to the floor.

Jesse James was buried at his childhood home in Clay County, Missouri. Because his mother feared that morbidly curious people would try to dig up his remains, Jesse's grave was placed

*After Jesse James's death in 1882, he became a
symbol of American restlessness.*

outside of Zerelda's bedroom window. She kept a careful eye on her son's burial site until her death in 1911.

The James farm is located in Kearney, Missouri, twenty-five miles northeast of Kansas City, Missouri, off Interstate 35.

John Ringo

d. 1882

"So you're the notorious Ringo Kid."
— ACTOR BERTON CHURCHILL TO JOHN WAYNE'S
CHARACTER JOHNNY RINGO IN THE MOVIE *STAGECOACH*, 1939

The desert Southwest in the late 1870s and early 1880s was teeming with desperados. The front pages of local daily newspapers from Bisbee, Arizona, to Las Cruces, New Mexico, listed the details of their crimes, and the publicity made a few of these outlaws famous. John Ringo was such a criminal.

Born John Peters Ringo on May 3, 1850, in Greenfork, Indiana, he was an educated man who attended William Jewell College in Liberty, Missouri. He was known to have quoted Shakespeare and read Latin. Not much is known of his early life. His parents, Martin and Mary, were farmers who relocated from Indiana to Missouri in 1856. The family pulled up stakes again in 1864 and headed for California. Martin was struggling with tuberculosis and hoped the Gold Country would bring him better health. The trip turned out to be a tragic adventure when Martin accidentally shot and killed himself en route. John and his mother continued west until they reached San Jose.

In 1869 John struck out on his own. He roamed about for

several years, never settling in any one place until he reached Burnett, Texas, in 1874. After being fined for firing his pistol in the town square, he was recruited by a vigilante group dedicated to the killing of cattle rustlers. Texas Rangers eventually apprehended John Ringo and another rider identified as the murderer of cattle thief Jim Cheyney.

A mob in favor of Ringo's actions broke him out of jail in January 1876, but he was quickly recaptured and imprisoned again. The case against Ringo was dismissed in court a year later, and he was set free. On the outside again he began keeping company with a gang of desperados that included John Wesley Hardin and Mannen Clements.

When the men parted ways in 1878, he

John Peters Ringo, 1850–1882

COURTESY OF ARIZONA HISTORICAL SOCIETY/TUCSON #78486

drifted west toward Tombstone, Arizona. On his way to the silver boomtown, he lingered for a while in Loyal Valley, Texas, and on November 5, 1878, he was elected as constable. By late 1879 he was back on the road to Arizona. Not long after he arrived in Tombstone, he befriended suspected cattle rustlers Ike and Billy Clanton and Tom McLaury.

COURTESY OF ARIZONA HISTORICAL SOCIETY/TUCSON #4940

*John Ringo's final resting place at the banks of
the Turkey Creek in southern Arizona.*

Ringo was involved in numerous saloon fights. His excessive drinking fueled his short temper, and when offended he would retaliate with his gun or fists. At the Crystal Palace Saloon in December 1879, he pistol-whipped a man for making a lewd comment to a woman and then shot the man in the throat.

John Ringo and outlaw Curly Bill Brocious were leaders of an anti-Earp force called the Cowboys. Wyatt, Virgil, and Morgan Earp were the law in Tombstone, and the cowboys were fiercely opposed to the lawmen's presence. After the gunfight at the OK Corral on October 26, 1881, Ringo was enraged at the Earps and Doc Holliday's so-called "murderous actions." Tensions grew between the characters and culminated in Ringo challenging Wyatt Earp to a gunfight. Seven months after calling Earp out, Ringo was found dead on the banks of the Turkey Creek in the foothills of the Chiricahua Mountains between Sierra Vista and Bisbee, Arizona.

A great deal of controversy surrounds the death of John Ringo. Some say he committed suicide after a long night of drinking; some maintain that fellow outlaw Buckskin Frank Leslie shot him. Others say Wyatt Earp killed him, and another faction believes it was Doc Holliday who did the deed.

John Ringo died on July 13, 1882, and his body was buried at the spot where he was found. His grave is marked by a large rock with his name scrawled across it along with the year of his death. Given John Ringo's close association with the cowboys involved in the gunfight at the OK Corral, the Arizona Historical Society decided to name the gunfighter's gravesite a state landmark.

James Marshall

d. 1885

"That James W. Marshall picked up the first piece of gold, is beyond doubt. Peter L. Weimer, who resides in this place, states positively that Mr. Marshall picked up the gold in his presence."
—THE COLOMA ARGUS NEWSPAPER, 1855

Prospectors and settlers were amazed at the ease with which gold was recovered among the rocks and streams of the California foothills in early 1848. The first gold was discovered by James Wilson Marshall, a carpenter by trade and former employee of Captain John A. Sutter. Marshall was wandering along the bank of the American River where he was building a sawmill when he noticed a peculiar golden stone in the bedrock. It was a find that changed the course of the history of the West.

James was born in Lambertville, New Jersey, in 1810, and from an early age he worked with his father learning the trade of carpentry, carriage making, and wheelwrighting. In 1828 he left home to start his own life. He settled in the Midwest, farming on land in Kansas, Indiana, and Illinois. Farming proved to be an unsuccessful venture for him, and in 1844 he headed west along the Oregon Trail to Puget Sound. Later he traveled down the

Sacramento River, arriving in California in 1845. He quickly found work at Sutter's Fort and in a short time had acquired several acres of land and livestock.

Toward the end of August 1847, Captain Sutter and James Marshall's working relationship had advanced beyond employer and employee, and they formed a partnership to build and operate a sawmill on a site fifty-four miles east of the fort. Marshall's part in the business was overseeing the actual construction and workings of the mill; Sutter supplied the capital to back the venture. Mr. P. L. Weimer and his family were hired on to accompany Marshall to the location to cook and labor for the builders constructing the mill. The building began around Christmas, and gold was discovered a little more than a month later. Marshall glanced down into the river water, and something caught his eye. He leaned forward to get a better look and saw something shining in the gravel. "Gold! Could it be gold?" he said to himself.

Marshall showed the rock to the workers around him. Many of them suspected the material to be iron pyrite, or fool's gold. Marshall decided to return to Sutter's Fort to verify the discovery. Before he left, he swore the mill workers to secrecy. In exchange for their silence, they would be given the chance to prospect on Sundays and after work.

As Marshall rode swiftly across the beautiful countryside toward the fort, he was troubled by a complication with the land where the gold was found. The property was purchased by Captain Sutter from Mexico and the local Indians, but since the sale of the land, California had become a territory of the United States. Marshall was concerned the United States government would not honor Sutter's prior claim once the gold strike was made public. When Marshall unveiled his findings to Sutter, Sutter was sure that the rock was gold, and he too was concerned about the claim. Marshall's hope was that the news of the discovery would be kept quiet long enough for Sutter to be granted full legal title with the new government. It was not to be, however. Marshall and Sutter's employees began to talk, sharing the news of the find with teamsters and trappers. Within six weeks of the discovery, Sutter's entire staff at the fort had deserted him, and Marshall's workers had abandoned the mill.

Marshall informed the new prospectors in the area that he and Sutter owned a twelve-mile tract of land along the riverbanks. He charged them 10 percent of their take for the privilege of working the gravel. His claim discouraged many miners, but when some of them made their way to San Francisco with full pockets, the rush was on. A band of frustrated miners who felt they were being denied access to the gold defied Marshall. They overtook the nearly completed mill and killed several men who sided with Marshall.

After being pushed off the stake that he found, Marshall left the area in disgust. He traveled around Northern California searching for another strike but was never fortunate enough to locate one. In 1857 Marshall returned to the Coloma area, where he bought some land and started a vineyard. High taxes and increased competition eventually drove him out of business.

In 1872 the California State Legislature awarded Marshall a two-year pension. The funds were in recognition of his role in the gold rush. The $200-a-year pension was renewed in 1874 and 1876 but lapsed in 1878.

James Marshall died a pauper on August 10, 1885, in Kelsey, California. He was seventy-three years old. He was buried in Coloma near the site of the vineyard he once owned. The monument atop his grave features a granite stature of Marshall pointing toward the place he found the glittery substance that dazzled a nation.

Aaron Augustus Sargent

d. 1887

*"The right of citizens of the United States to vote shall
not be denied or abridged . . . on account of sex."*
—AARON A. SARGENT, 1878

Among the pioneers who helped California graduate from the wild
days of a gold rush territory into a civilized state was Senator
Aaron Augustus Sargent. The former cabinetmaker arrived in the
mining camp called Nevada in 1849 and was moderately successful in his search for gold. He then became a partner with several
others in the *Nevada Journal* newspaper.

Sargent was born on September 28, 1827, in Newburyport,
Massachusetts, and in his teens moved to Philadelphia and worked
as a printer. In 1847 he moved to Washington, D.C., where he was
a secretary to a congressman. His background in government
helped lay the groundwork for the political life ahead.

Three years after his arrival in California, Sargent built a small
frame house in the center of Nevada City for his fiancée, Ellen
Clark. He and Ellen were sweethearts in their youth, and he had
promised to return for her once he had made a life for them out
west. The pair married in March 1852 and settled into their new
home by October.

While Ellen was creating a comfortable home, Aaron was busy vigorously presenting the political campaign in the California newspaper he now solely owned. He favored the policies of the Whigs and the early Republican-style party. An opposing point of view was enthusiastically espoused by a newspaper called *Young America*, which heralded the views of the Democrats.

Ellen worried in 1853 when the printed attacks on her husband became so heated he expected to be challenged to a duel. However, a friend, Judge David S. Belden, came to Aaron's defense before a challenge was issued. Editor R. A. Davridge of *Young America* was threatening to shoot Aaron because of his strong political views. A crowd gathered. Judge Belden stepped in, drew his pistol, and announced he wanted to give a demonstration of his shooting skills. Using cards as targets, Belden shot rapidly until the gun was empty, hitting a card with each shot.

He then announced he'd be happy to talk to anyone who didn't like Aaron Sargent, a man who had a family, which he himself did not, and thus had nothing to lose if the discussion ended in the exchange of bullets. No one accepted.

In the summer of 1852, Sargent pursued a law degree and was admitted to the California bar in 1854. Shortly afterwards he opened his own practice in Nevada City and eventually became the county's district attorney.

While Aaron was making his mark on the legal and political world, his wife was raising their two children and building her own quiet legend. In addition to founding the first women's suffrage group in Nevada City in 1869, she served as president of similar organizations and presided at conventions called to gather women together to encourage them to continue the fight for the right to vote.

Fiery abolitionists and early feminist Susan B. Anthony visited the Sargent home in 1871. As a young Quaker, Susan

Anthony had worked in the antislavery movement until passage of the Fourteenth Amendment in 1863 banned slavery in the United States. With that victory she turned her attention to another case of unjust treatment in a land where all were said to be created equal—women's rights. At that time in history, Susan, Ellen, and Aaron were three of the nation's biggest supporters of women's rights.

When Aaron was elected to the U.S. Senate, the Sargent family moved to Washington, D.C. At the end of his term in the Senate, he was elected to the 37th, 41st, and 42nd Congresses and served in that capacity for more than ten years. In 1861 he was the author of the 1st Pacific Railroad Act, an act to aid in the construction of a railroad and telegraph line from the Missouri River to the Pacific Ocean.

Sargent's most controversial political move occurred in 1877 when he introduced a revision to the constitution

Aaron Augustus Sargent,
1827–1887

that would give women the right to vote. The Nineteenth Amendment was ratified in 1920, forty-three years after it was introduced.

Sargent retired from politics in 1883 and resumed his law practice in San Francisco. He passed away on August 14, 1887, from heart failure and was interred at the Laurel Hill Cemetery. When the cemetery was moved to make room for more buildings,

PHOTOGRAPH BY CYNTHIA MARTIN

The tomb of Aaron Sargent—journalist, politician, and miner

Sargent's remains were brought back to Nevada City. In 1888 his ashes were scattered over his Quaker Hill mining claim and his vault was moved to a new location as a monument to his pioneering deeds. Aaron Sargent's grave marker is now located at the Pioneer Cemetery in Nevada City, California.

Aaron's gracious and determined wife, Ellen, died in 1911. She too was buried in the San Francisco Laurel Hill Cemetery, and more than a thousand people attended her graveside service. The mayor of San Francisco ordered all flags flown at half-staff in her honor.

Doc Holliday

d. 1887

"He was very much disliked and under the influence of liquor was a most dangerous man."

—LAWMAN-TURNED-SPORTSWRITER
BAT MASTERSON'S THOUGHTS ABOUT DENTIST-
TURNED-GUNFIGHTER DOC HOLLIDAY

He was as charming and beguiling as he was fearless and deadly. He was the most well-known doctor in the Old West and behaved more like an outlaw and less like a gentlemen dentist from Georgia. Doc Holliday was a skilled gunfighter who preferred gambling to any other profession.

John Henry Holliday was born to Alice Jane McKey and Henry Burroughs Holliday on August 14, 1851, in the tiny town of Griffin, Georgia. He attended the finest schools for the sons of southern gentlemen. In his free time he roamed the woods around town, learning the ways of the wilderness. He also took up pistol practice and was an excellent marksman by the time he was fourteen years old.

His life changed in 1866 when his mother died from tuberculosis. She had been a stabilizing force in his life, and with her death came a melancholy that he would carry with him to his grave. Relations between John and his father were strained when

Henry married a twenty-year-old woman three months after his wife's funeral. John shot a Union soldier in an altercation over a watering hole shortly after the wedding. In an attempt to protect his son, John's father sent him to dental college in Pennsylvania. Henry threw off bounty hunters looking for John by telling them his son was attending school in Baltimore.

John graduated in 1872 and returned home with a strange cough. He was diagnosed as having tuberculosis. Doctors told him that he wouldn't live six months in Georgia and suggested he move to Texas, where the climate was better. Just before he moved he attended the funeral of his brother, who had died of the same ailment.

Shortly after his brother's death, Holliday, now a dignified six-foot-tall, twenty-one-year-old with blue-gray eyes and a thick mustache, left home and headed for Fort Griffith, Texas. When he arrived, he met a young prostitute named Kate Elder. The two were involved in an on-again-off-again romance that lasted fifteen years.

Doc toured the Western territories working at times as a dentist, but mostly earning his keep playing cards. He traveled the boomtowns of Dallas, Denver, Pueblo, Leadville, Dodge City, Tucson, and Tombstone. Any man foolish enough to suggest Doc acquired his poker winnings by being less than honest was quickly and violently corrected. Doc was as proficient with a knife as he was a gun. He never shied away from a fight, and he shot or killed any man who challenged him.

Outside of his paramour Kate Elder, or Big Nose Kate as she was more commonly known, Holliday's only friends were legendary lawmen Bat Masterson and Wyatt Earp. While in Kansas the three men played nightly card games and drank. According to another well-known western figure, Bat Masterson, "Doc idolized Wyatt." The hotheaded and impetuous Holliday studied Earp's

John Henry "Doc" Holliday, 1851–1887

COURTESY ARZONA HISTORICAL SOCIETY/TUCSON #12169

unflinching demeanor and mannerisms and made sure his gun hand was available whenever Wyatt needed help.

By 1874 Doc and Kate had settled in Las Vegas, New Mexico. The two were living as husband and wife and were making a good living—Doc as a gambler and Kate as the owner of a parlor house. Their lives were chaotic and tumultuous. Doc had frequent altercations with the law. He gunned down competitors and was implicated in the holdup of a stage. His tuberculosis worsened and disagreements with Kate increased. After two years in the same location, Doc decided to accept an offer from his brothers to move to Tombstone. Kate objected to Doc leaving their home and refused to go along with him at first, but within a month she followed him. Both arrived in the silver boomtown in early 1881.

Doc's health continued to decline; he was thin and pale. His bright eyes faded into a cold, hard gray, and his head was now topped by enough white hairs to make his hair appear ash blond. Alcoholism further deteriorated his personality, and his hangovers were marvels to behold.

Doc and Kate were residing at Fly's Boarding House when the gunfight at the OK Corral occurred. Ike Clanton and members of a cattle-rustling gang of outlaws feuding with the Earps had threatened Wyatt and his brothers. The altercation resulted in the deaths of three men. After the gunfight and the subsequent vendetta ride in which the cowboy outlaws were tracked down and killed, Doc headed for Colorado. In Pueblo he became a fixture in the gaming room of the Comique Club. Most of the gamblers, bartenders, and police knew about his part in the OK Corral "street fight" and regarded him as something of a celebrity.

In 1884 Doc was in and out of sanitariums in an attempt to help his lungs, but the disease had progressed beyond repair. His penchant for getting in trouble did not falter in spite of his physical condition. He had run-ins with the law for crimes committed in Kansas and was arrested for shooting a Leadville bartender.

By the spring of 1887, Doc Holliday was a patient at the Glenwood Springs Health Spa in Glenwood, Colorado. He was emaciated and frail, and his body was shaken by constant coughing spells. He would not leave the facility alive.

On November 8, 1887, after he asked a nurse to give him a drink of whiskey and to find his boots, Doc's breathing became extremely labored. By the time his boots were located, Holliday was taking his last breath. Looking down at his bare feet before closing his eyes, he said, "Well, I'll be damned." He had always insisted he would die with his boots on.

Doc Holliday is buried at the Pioneer Cemetery in Glenwood Springs, Colorado. The words on this tombstone read: DOC HOLLIDAY 1852–1887. HE DIED IN BED.

Sarah Winnemucca

d. 1891

"In the history of the Indians she and Pocahontas will be principal female characters, and her singular devotion to her race will no doubt be chronicled as an illustration of the better traits of Indian Character."
— SAN FRANCISCO CALL, JANUARY 1885

The Piute Indian Sarah Winnemucca listened intently as one of the tribe's elders told the story of how the army soldiers killed a party of their people on a fishing expedition. Relations between the Piutes and white settlers had been strained since the discovery of silver in northern Nevada in 1859. An influx of prospectors and their families onto tribal land threatened the Piutes' way of life. The 1865 massacre of a Piute fishing party by United States troops had further fueled problems. Among the dead that day was Sarah's infant brother. Hearing details of the incident made the well-known Piute leader sad but more determined than ever to travel to Washington and inform the powers there of the difficulties.

Sarah was born in 1844 in Washoe County, Nevada. Her grandfather was Chief Truckee, a former guide who assisted white explorers, such as John C. Fremont, in finding their way over the

Sierra Nevadas. The friendly Chief Truckee could not have foreseen the multitudes of white settlers who would descend upon the area and force him and his people out.

"I was a very small child when the first white people came into our country," Sarah shared in her autobiography. "They came like a lion, yes, like a roaring lion and have continued ever since, and I have never forgotten their first coming."

Sarah's grandfather was a wise man who recognized the importance of making peace with the newcomers. Wanting his grandchildren to have every advantage in dealing with these new inhabitants, he arranged for Sarah and her sister to learn English and the white man's way of life. A Virginia trader and his family who lived at a nearby settlement served as the girls' teachers.

Sarah was a quick study and extremely bright. She was particularly gifted in language. By the time she was fourteen years old, she could speak five different languages, including English and Spanish. At her grandfather's urging, Sarah continued her education at a convent school in San Jose, California.

During her long absence the situation between the Piute Indians and the white pioneers grew worse. The Piutes were being completely crowded out, and as their food source had been nearly depleted by the hordes of emigrants, they had been driven to work menial jobs to purchase supplies. The Piutes were then forced to move to a reservation near Pyramid Lake, Nevada. When white squatters moved in on the lake, the government again pushed the Piutes off the land, this time sending them to a reservation in Oregon.

Sarah was brokenhearted over what seemed like the inevitable demise of the great tribe and wanted to help preserve what little was left. In 1871, at the age of twenty-seven, she took a job with the Bureau of Indian Affairs at Fort McDermitt in Oregon. Sarah was able to serve her people at the Malheur Indian Reservation by

Sarah Winnemucca, 1844–1891

teaching school and issuing supplies. Sarah was married twice in the first four years she was employed at the reservation. Her first husband was a lieutenant in the army who drank a lot. Her second husband was an Indian whom she left because he was abusive.

A new Indian agent was selected to oversee the events at Malheur reservation in 1878. Sarah has worked with the new agent prior to his appointment and knew him to be corrupt and self-serving. When she conveyed her opinion to the authorities, she was promptly fired as the reservation interpreter. The government's decision to ignore her comments and relieve her of her position infuriated her, and she decided to take the matter to the officials in Washington, D.C. While en route, she found herself in the middle of a war between the Bannock Indians of Idaho Territory and the U.S. government.

The Piutes were caught in a vise between the Bannock Indians, their northern neighbors in Idaho and Oregon, and the increasing number of settlers pushing them out of their tribal lands in Nevada. A Bannock war party had captured a band of Piute, including Sarah's father, Winnemucca, now the chief of the Piute tribe. Sarah quickly volunteered her interpretive services to the army. They accepted her offer and sent her out with two Indian guides to locate the Bannock Indians holding her father and the others. Sarah and her companions traveled more than two hundred miles before finding Chief Winnemucca and the other Piutes. Disguised as a brave, Sarah managed to sneak into the Bannock camp and rescue her father and her people.

In 1880 Sarah finally reached the nation's capital and was allowed to speak with the secretary of the interior and President Rutherford B. Hayes about the treatment of Native Americans. The government made promises for improvement but ultimately did not keep them. The broken promises reflected back on Sarah and eroded away at the trust the Piute placed in her.

Despite the U.S. government's betrayal and the lack of confidence her people had in her efforts, she worked hard for them and dedicated her life to the cause. In 1881 Sarah married for a third time. That marriage, like the others, ended in divorce. She lectured across the nation, started a school for Indian children, and wrote the first book ever penned by a Native woman. Her book, *Life Among the Piutes, Their Wrongs and Claims,* was first published in 1883.

The original editor of the book, Mary Peabody Mann, noted that Sarah's speeches were extraordinarily moving, but that it was Sarah's goal to set down in writing the full story. "It is the first outbreak of the American Indian in human literature, and it has a single aim—to tell the truth as it lies in the heart of a true patriot, and one whose knowledge of the two races gives her an opportunity of comparing them justly."

Years of marital hardship and personal loss took a toll on Sarah's emotional and physical well-being. At the age of forty-seven, she developed a persistent cough and was suffering from extreme exhaustion. She felt dejected and isolated by her native people and the United States government, and this further contributed to her declining health.

Sarah Winnemucca passed away on October 17, 1891, while visiting her sister in Bozeman, Montana. The cause of death was tuberculosis. Since her passing, her work as an author has been recognized by the University of Nevada, and she has been inducted into the Nevada Writer's Hall of Fame. An elementary school in Washoe County, Nevada, was named in her honor, and in 2005 a statue of the tireless crusader for Indian rights was erected at the U.S. Capitol.

Although Sarah made great strides to liberate Native Americans from their "white enemies," she died believing she was a failure. She is buried in an unmarked grave at Henry's Flat in Nez Perce County, Idaho.

Bob Ford

d. 1892

"Instantly his real purpose flashed upon my mind. I knew I had not fooled him. He was too sharp for that. He knew at that moment as well as I did that I was there to betray him."

— BOB FORD'S ACCOUNT OF THE EVENTS LEADING
UP TO HIS KILLING JESSE JAMES, APRIL 1882

Dressed in his finest Sunday suit, Bob Ford struck a proud pose for an eager photographer in Pueblo, New Mexico. A brilliant flash lit up the photographer's studio, and when the smoke from the phosphorous lens disappeared, a clear view of the outlaw Ford could be seen. His tailor-made suit was accentuated by a brocaded vest and diamond stickpin. In his left hand he held the pistol he used to kill Jesse James.

From the moment Ford gunned down the legendary James on April 3, 1882, he had been boasting of his deed. In fact less than an hour after the murder, Bob Ford and his brother Charlie had hurried to a telegraph office and sent a message to the governor of Missouri with news that Jesse James was dead. "I have killed Jesse James," the wire read. The brutal act entitled him to a substantial reward.

Robert Newton Ford, 1862–1892

Bob Ford was born in Ray County, Missouri, in 1862. He was a troubled youth who wanted nothing more than to be an outlaw. His heroes were renegades who robbed banks and trains. He longed to meet Cole Younger and Jesse James, and in 1879 he got his chance. Bob and his younger brother, Charlie, joined James's gang and accompanied them on several raids. It wasn't long before Bob graduated from robbery to murder.

In January 1882 authorities learned he had shot a fellow gang member in the head and buried his body in a shallow grave. To avoid prosecution, Ford struck a deal with Missouri governor Thomas Crittenden that involved Jesse James. Ford would receive a full pardon if he killed the elusive outlaw.

In early April 1882 Ford seized the opportunity to kill the notorious James. Bob and Charlie were with Jesse at his home discussing plans for another robbery when Jesse turned his back on the brothers. A bullet from Bob's six-shooter crashed through Jesse's skull.

News of Ford's act spread quickly. Many Missouri residents called the boys cowards and made their time at home in Ray County miscrable. To make matters worse for the brothers, it was rumored that Frank James was going to be coming for them to get revenge for Jesse's death. Charlie was petrified and fled the area hoping to avoid the backlash. His nerves finally got the better of him, however, and he committed suicide.

In spite of the jeers and shouts of recrimination and threats of death from those who believed killing Jesse James was an act of treason, Bob continued to be vocal about the shooting. In order to deal with the criticism he encountered, he began drinking to excess and gambling away his money. He traveled constantly, hoping to outrun anyone who wanted him dead for what he did. He met his demise in Pueblo, New Mexico, on June 8, 1892. He was involved in an altercation with a man he claimed had stolen a diamond ring from him. When Bob wouldn't retract the accusation, the man shot and killed him.

PHOTOGRAPH BY CYNTHIA MARTIN

BOB FORD

DEC. 8, 1841 – JUNE 8, 1892

THE MAN WHO SHOT JESSE JAMES

Initially buried in Crede, Colorado, Bob Ford's
remains were moved to Richmond, Missouri. Although the tombstone
indicates he was born in 1841, the actual year of birth was 1862.

Ford's body was returned to Missouri and buried in the family plot at the Ray County Cemetery in Richmond, Missouri. A rock with Ford's name on it marks the site of his grave. Signs that read HERE LIES THE DIRTY LITTLE COWARD WHO SHOT MISTER HOWARD, (James's alias at the time of his death) are occasionally found propped against the stone.

Sheriff David Douglass

d. 1896

"I knew him well and I considered him one of the bravest men I ever met. He did not know what fear was and his one idea while in performance of his duty was to get his man."

— SACRAMENTO SHERIFF TOM O'NEILL'S REMEMBRANCE
OF SLAIN SHERIFF DAVID DOUGLASS, JULY 1896

Pioneers lured west by promises of great fortune encountered rough terrain, inclement weather, hostile Natives, and highway robbers. Their survival depended on a variety of things, not the least of which were lawmen. The local sheriff and his deputies made sure settlers were protected from thieves and murderers threatening to overtake them on the trails and in the gold rush mining camps. One lawman who attempted to do just that was David F. Douglass.

Douglass was elected to the post of Nevada County sheriff in 1894. Sheriff Douglass had been a guard for gold shipments traveling by train and had also served as a messenger for Wells Fargo. He was known by residents in Grass Valley and Nevada City, California, as a bold, fearless, and defiant officer, dedicated to making sure the law was upheld.

*David F. Douglass, a Nevada County, California, sheriff
died in the line of duty in 1896.*

On Sunday, July 26, 1896, Douglass set out after an outlaw named C. Meyers who had been terrorizing the county. The pursuit ended in the death of the bandit and the sheriff. Sheriff Douglass shot and killed the highwaymen, but just who shot Douglass remains a mystery.

After learning where the thief was hiding out, Douglass mounted his horse and took out after him. When the sheriff hadn't returned by the next day, his friends and deputies combed the area looking for him. His body was discovered a few feet from the outlaw's. Cedar and chaparral trees were thick around the secluded scene, and it was evident to the sheriff's deputies that he had been lured to the spot.

Sheriff Douglass's body was found with his head pointing downhill, his face plunged in the brush and dirt. *The Grass Valley Union* newspaper reported that the "force of the fall brought a slight contusion to the forehead." Those who discovered his body believed that the bullet that took his life had entered his back, thrusting him forward. The report quoted deputies as saying, "Undoubtedly Sheriff Douglass had shot Meyers dead and was going to inspect the damage when a bullet pierced his frame."

As subsequent facts developed it appeared there had been an accomplice of Meyers hiding somewhere in the area. The unknown shooter fired shots at Douglass. The first bullet went into his back on the left side, and the second hit him in the right hand. Nevada County residents were shocked by the news of the respected sheriff's death. They arrived in droves at the scene of the tragedy hoping to find a clue as to who the murderer might have been. Dozens of well-armed men scoured the hills in search of the assassin. The killer was never found.

A monument to the memory of the sheriff and the outlaw (buried at the site) was erected at the location of the tragic gunfight in early 1900.

PHOTOGRAPH BY CYNTHIA MARTIN

The tombstone reads: "Sheriff David Fulton Douglass. On this spot Sheriff Douglass, a native son of the golden West, gave his life. July 26, 1896. Bravely performing his duty, alone he tracked a highwayman to this retreat and both fell in battle."

It is believed Douglass was pitted against two and then one escaped. The bodies were lying parallel to one another. The gravestone over Sheriff Douglass's grave and that of the bandit he shot is located in the Tahoe National Forest in Nevada City, California, on a dirt pathway on Old Airport Road.

Nancy Kelsey

d. 1896

"Once, I remember, when I was struggling along . . .
I looked back and saw Missus Benjamin Kelsey a little
ways behind me, with her child in her arms, barefooted,
I think, and leading a horse . . . It was a sight I shall
never forget."

— NICHOLAS DAWSON, A MEMBER OF
THE BIDWELL-BARTLESON PARTY, 1841

At eighteen years old, Nancy Kelsey became the first white woman to cross the Sierra Nevadas. The teenager made the long trip overland barefoot with a one-year old baby on her hip. Born in Barren County, Kentucky, in 1823, she married Benjamin L. Kelsey when she was fifteen. She had fallen in love with his restless, adventurous spirit, and from the day the two exchanged vows she could not imagine her life without him. At the age of seventeen, Nancy agreed to follow Benjamin to a strange new land rumored to be a place where a "poor man could prosper." Nancy, Benjamin, and their daughter, Ann, arrived in Spalding Grove, Kansas, just in time to join the first organized group of American settlers traveling to California by land. The train was organized and led by John

Nancy Kelsey, 1823–1896

Bidwell, a New York school teacher, and John Bartleson, a land speculator and wagon master.

Nancy's recollections of some of the other members of the Bidwell-Bartleson Party and the apprehension she felt about the trip were recorded in the *San Francisco Examiner* in 1893. She described what it was like when the wagon train first set out on May 12, 1841: "A man by the name of Fitzpatrick was our pilot, and we had a priest with us who was bound for the northwest coast to teach the Flathead Indians. We numbered thirty-three all told and I was the only woman. I had a baby to take care of too."

By July the emigrant party had made it to Fort Laramie, Wyoming. The party experienced little trouble on the first twelve hundred miles of the trip, but the difficulties they faced on their travels from Wyoming into California more than made up for that. While resting near the Platte River, one of the members of their wagon train was taken captive by Indians. He was later released, but the Indians never strayed far from the group.

The Indians' constant presence made the livestock nervous and frightened Nancy and her baby. Benjamin recognized that his wife was fearful and stayed close by her side. Whenever she wanted to turn back, he would urge her on by quoting the notices about California that he had read in the Western Emigration Society paper. They called California "a land of perennial spring and boundless fertility." Nancy's daydreams about the life they would have there sustained her for a time, but eventually her worst fears were realized.

By August the Bidwell-Bartleson Party was completely lost. They knew they were supposed to be near the Humboldt River, but it was nowhere in sight. Food was scarce, and the animals became too exhausted to pull the wagons. Still, the party pushed west, abandoning their wagons one by one and slaughtering their oxen for food.

On September 7, 1841, the weary group located the Humboldt River, but then they could not find the road that would lead from there to the Truckee River. Nancy held her daughter tightly in her arms and desperately tried to shade her from the sun. Her baby was hungry and cried to be fed, but food was again running short. In October the party killed the last of their oxen. The weather turned cold, and Nancy longed to go back home, but the party continued on until they came face-to-face with several high peaks.

Later, Nancy recalled the struggle through the jagged mountains that appeared to be "capped with snow, perhaps of a thousand years. We had a difficult time finding a way down the mountains. At one time I was left alone for nearly half a day, and I was afraid of Indians, I sat all the while with my baby on my lap. It seemed to me while I was there alone that the moaning of the winds through the pines was the loneliest sound I had ever heard."

Nancy was an inspiration to her fellow travelers. Many of them kept journals in which they wrote about her bravery and made mention of the fact that her baby was never sick a day of the trip. In 1842 Joseph Chiles, one of the members of the party, wrote about Nancy's courage and strength: "She bore the fatigues of the journey with so much heroism, patience, and kindness that there still exists a warmth in every heart for the mother and her child."

Nancy Kelsey's pioneering days did not end once she made it over the Sierra Nevadas. She had hoped Benjamin would settle down and build a life for her and their daughter, Ann, but after five months of being in California, he decided to move the family to Oregon. Nancy didn't want to go, but she was dedicated to her husband.

In 1847 Benjamin and Nancy traveled from Oregon to the Napa Valley, the San Joaquin plains, and Mendocino. Benjamin left

Nancy alone in 1848 to see if there was any truth to the gold rumors. He was gone ten days and brought back one thousand dollars. The next time he went to the mines he took a flock of sheep up for mutton and brought back sixteen thousand dollars. He used the money to buy Nancy and, by this time, their two daughters, a lake ranch in a town the couple had helped build called Kelseyville.

Nancy was finally living the good life her husband had promised her, but it was short-lived. Benjamin sold the lake ranch after a few months and took his family down the Humboldt River to be among the first settlers of Eureka and Arcata. Just when Nancy thought they would finally stay put, Benjamin came down with tuberculosis, and they were compelled to travel to a drier location for his health.

In 1874 Nancy followed Benjamin back to California. He built her a cabin high up in the Cuyama Mountains in San Diego. He died in Los Angeles in 1888. Nancy died of cancer in 1896. Her grave in Santa Barbara is marked by a rock. The simple inscription on it reads KELSEY.

The Lone Angel
1897

A demur marble angel sits among the faded wooded crosses and weather-ravaged rock grave memorials at the Odd Fellows Cemetery in Bodie, California. The three-foot cherub holds a flower wreath in her left hand and rests her hand on her right elbow. The lone angel watches over the burial site of a three-year-old little girl named Evelyn Meyers.

Evelyn was the joyful, precocious daughter of Fannie and Albert Meyers. Born in Bodie on May 1, 1894, the child had a ready smile for everyone she saw and a particular fondness for an elderly miner who was a dear friend of the family.

Fannie would take Evelyn with her when she went to do the weekly shopping. The little girl played outside with the other children in town and sat with the old miner friend and listened to the stories he would tell. Evelyn would follow the man everywhere he went, from the blacksmith shop to the church. The miner was taken with the little girl's devotion.

In the spring of 1897, Evelyn spotted the miner on Main Street and took out after him. Unaware that the child was following him, the man made his way to his claim just outside the town. Evelyn crept quietly behind. Whistling and preoccupied with the job of searching for gold, the miner raised a pickax up and back to begin chipping away at a rock wall. He still did not know Evelyn was behind him as he began to work. The top of the pickax caught

Evelyn Meyers's tombstone in Bodie, California, is one of a handful of marble markers among hundreds of wooden ones.

the girl in the head, killing her instantly. The miner was devastated. The girl was laid to rest on April 6, 1897.

Thousands of Bodie visitors have passed by the angel tombstone in the one-hundred-plus years it has been standing in the cemetery. Vandals have broken the top of the wings on the statue as well as the left foot. The inscription at the base of the marble is still clearly visible and reads BELOVED DAUGHTER.

The Odd Fellows Cemetery is located east of Bodie.

John Bidwell
d. 1900

*"The party whose fortunes I have followed across
the plains was not only the first that went direct to
California from the East; we were probably the first
white people, except Bonneville's party of 1833, that
ever crossed the Sierras."*
—JOHN BIDWELL, DECEMBER 1890

Among the many brave men who ventured into the remote lands
of America's Western territories to establish a trail to the Pacific
Coast was politician and military leader John Bidwell. At the age
of twenty-one, Bidwell joined the first wagon-train expedition to
California. The intrepid former schoolteacher, along with a handful of other men on the journey, crossed the Sierra Mountain range
into the Sacramento Valley in November 1841.

Shortly after the pioneer's arrival, he took a job at Sutter's
Fort working for the founder of the outpost, John A. Sutter.
Bidwell was Sutter's chief clerk and was given the monumental
duty of stocking the facility with supplies ranging from fruits and
vegetables to cannons and ammunition.

Bidwell was born on August 5, 1819, in Chautauqua County,
New York. His formative years were spent in Pennsylvania and

Ohio. He was educated at various country schools and later attended the Kingville Academy in Ohio, where he decided to become a teacher. After hearing about the wonders of California, Bidwell decided to leave teaching behind and go west. He helped form the Western Emigration Society and recruited settlers to accompany him overland.

John Bidwell, 1819–1900

Not only was Bidwell a stalwart trailblazer and capable business manager, but he was a successful prospector as well. He discovered gold along the Feather River and used the funds made from the Bidwell Bar find to purchase a twenty-thousand-acre plantation he named Rancho Chico.

After serving two years in the army, fighting in the Mexican-American war and rising in rank to general, Bidwell left the military and returned to his home in Northern California. When he wasn't managing the growing of crops and caring for the livestock on his property, he was involved in political pursuits. In 1849 he was elected to the California Senate. In 1850 and 1860 he was the state supervisor for the United States census. He served as a delegate for the Democratic Party's national convention held in 1860, was a delegate for the Republican Party convention in 1864 and 1865, and served a two-year term in Congress.

U.S. Congressman John Bidwell was buried
in Butte County in April 1900.

On April 16, 1868, he married Annie Ellicott Kennedy, whom he met during one of his visits to Washington, D.C. Present at their wedding were Presidents Andrew Johnson and Ulysses S. Grant. The couple lived the bulk of their married life at Rancho Chico, working their prize-winning orchards and providing financial assistance to the community at large.

John Bidwell ran for the office of governor on two different occasions, but failed both times to get elected. In 1890 he was the Prohibition candidate for president of the United States.

The respected statesman died on April 4, 1900. He had been clearing brush along Chico Creek when he suffered a heart attack. The last words he is known to have said were to his wife the morning he left to begin the chore. He told her, "I feel like a young boy."

John Bidwell was laid to rest at the Chico Cemetery in Chico, California. Hundreds throughout the state attended his funeral. Children from the Mechoopda Indian Reservation, located on Bidwell's land, tossed wildflowers and garden blossoms over his grave. The service ended with a chorus of mourners singing traditional religious hymns.

John's wife, Annie, honored her husband's last request, which was to donate more than two thousand acres of their ranch to the city of Chico to be used exclusively as a public park. Bidwell Park is now one of the largest city parks in the West.

Old Joe

d. 1901

"The wagon rests in winter; the sleigh in summer; the horse never."

—Yiddish Proverb

On a hot July day at the turn of the century, an old teamster stood over the grave of his best friend and offered up a prayer. The inscription scrawled across the crude tombstone simply read OLD JOE. DIED JULY 3, 1901. It stood alone next to the well-traveled road leading to the mining town of Foresthill, California, and it is still standing today.

In the early 1850s prospectors and stage drivers traveled the well-worn route known as Foresthill Road from the mining town of Auburn into the gold rush camp in and around Foresthill. Many pioneers and miners lost their lives in the area that yielded millions of dollars in gold. Old Joe was one of them. The teamster who buried his friend no doubt wept at his loss. Most assume the plot belongs to an Indian or early settler, but it actually belongs to an animal.

Old Joe was a stagecoach horse who sacrificed his life in an attempt to carry through to safety passengers and supplies entrusted to him. He was fatally wounded by a shot from a holdup man's

PHOTOGRAPH BY CYNTHIA MARTIN

*Tourists frequently visit Old Joe's tombstone,
leaving flowers and flags on the grave.*

gun when the stage driver refused to halt. He died with his harness
on. His body was dragged to the side of the road he had trekked
day after day and buried.

The stage robbery was the last one on the line. A young man
who was a resident of Foresthill was arrested and charged with the
crime sometime afterward. Years later the Wells Fargo box that was
carried away from the scene of the crime was found in the
American River Canyon.

A large black oak, behind which the holdup man stood while
awaiting the approach of the stage, still stands as a sentinel over
Old Joe's grave. When the bandit shot Old Joe, driver Henry
Crockett, in spite of the shotgun leveled at him by the bandit, did
not mince words in expressing his rage. "You've killed the best
horse in this country and you'll pay for it, by God," he shouted.

Death came close to Crockett that day, but it had to wait for a railroad train at a depot near Sacramento. Crockett was struck by a fast passenger engine several years later and died shortly thereafter. Unlike his traveling companion Old Joe, Crockett's burial site is not known.

Old Joe's grave is located along U.S. Highway 101 North, seven miles south of Auburn, California.

Calamity Jane

d. 1902

"Though she did not do a man's share of the heavy work, she has gone in places where old frontiersmen were unwilling to trust themselves, and her courage and good-fellowship made her popular with every man in the command."

— One of many comments Buffalo Bill Cody had about the amazing life of Calamity Jane, given to a Rocky Mountain newspaper reporter in 1906

Among the many mourners who attended the legendary Wild Bill Hickok's funeral on August 3, 1876, was a sorrowful, rough-looking woman clad in buckskins and a weathered cowboy hat. Her name was Martha Jane Canary-Burke, better known as Calamity Jane. She was as famous as the lawmen-gunfighter whose grave she was sobbing over. The nontraditional lifestyle she lived earned her the reputation as a woman who always did as she pleased. She was an army scout, a railroad worker, stage-coach driver, wagon freighter, Indian fighter, nurse, and some-times a prostitute. Jane could drink the average man under the table and cuss with the best of them. For most of her adult life, she was devoted to one man, Bill Hickok.

Calamity Jane was born in Princeton, Missouri, in 1852. From an early age she fought the idea that little girls should always dress like proper ladies and excel at domestic chores like cooking and sewing. Jane liked to run with the boys and roam the countryside on her horse. She was twelve years old when her family headed west, and she was excited about the promising adventure that laid ahead. She fell in love with the wild country, and when she wasn't riding the range she was holed up in a cow town watching the gamblers, miners, ranch hands, and ladies of the night come and go from the saloons and dance halls. Little did she know at the time how important those establishments would be in her future.

She was thirteen years old when both her parents passed away. Her mother, Charlotte, died en route to the gold diggings in Montana. Her father, Robert, died a year later. As the oldest of six siblings, Calamity was left to care for the family. In 1867 she moved the Canary offspring to Fort Bridger, Wyoming. She kept her brothers and sister fed by working as a laundress and by working as a prostitute at a local brothel.

In 1870 Jane left the hard life she'd been living and drifted across the Wyoming territory. According to her autobiography she ended up in Fort Russell, Wyoming, and signed on as a scout for General George Custer. Her skills as a tracker and hunter made her a natural for the position. It was the first of many frontier jobs the independent woman would sign on to do.

Calamity Jane's employment aspirations were as unconventional as her manner of dress. She wore men's clothing, complete with long underwear and boots, and sported a pair of six-shooters on her hips. Her unusual style and ability to master jobs traditionally done by men, made her a popular western character and earned her the handle that became legend. Tales of her adventures found their way into dime novels published in the East and

Martha Jane Canary Burke, 1852–1902

Calamity Jane was in love with Wild Bill Hickok most of her life. She was laid to rest beside him in the summer of 1876.

helped make her a household name across the country.

Over her fifty-plus years, she traveled from the Dakotas to Arizona and back again. In spite of her hard drinking and bawdy ways, she was a compassionate soul who on more than one occasion helped care for ailing miners dying of smallpox.

Jane kept company with various men from time to time and was even married once, but her heart belonged to James Butler Hickok. They arrived in Deadwood, South Dakota, in 1876 and were frequently seen together. Hickok maintained the pair were only friends, but Jane insisted they were more. Whatever their relationship might have been, it's clear that Jane was dedicated to Wild Bill. She grieved for months after he was killed.

On August 1, 1902, seventeen years after Hickok died, Calamity Jane passed away from pneumonia while staying at the

Callaway Hotel in Terry, South Dakota. She was fifty-one. Her body was returned to Deadwood, where the town undertaker outfitted her in a white cotton dress before placing her in a cloth-lined coffin.

According to the *Black Hills Daily Times,* Jane's funeral was "one of the largest Deadwood had ever seen." Mourners paraded past her casket, remembering with fondness Calamity's character. One resident who felt the once-feisty woman did not look natural placed a pair of six-shooters in each of her hands. The undertaker removed the weapons and chastised viewers about disturbing the body. His pleas went ignored, and many in attendance cut locks of her hair off to keep as souvenirs. The man was finally forced to build a wire cage over the corpse in order to prevent further such action.

Calamity Jane's last request to be buried next to Wild Bill was honored. Before she was laid to rest beside the man she loved at the Mount Moriah Cemetery in Deadwood, Seth Bullock—lawman, politician, and Jane's friend—delivered her eulogy.

Two names are inscribed on the tombstone standing over Jane's grave. One reads CALAMITY JANE and the other MARTHA JANE BURKE.

Nellie Pooler Chapman

d. 1906

"My chair is a barrel cut in this wise, with a stick with headrest attached. The lower half of the barrel stuffed firmly with pine needles and covered with a strong potato sack over which I had an elegant cover of striped calico."
—J. FOSTER FLAG, FORTY-NINER DENTIST

Petite Nellie Pooler Chapman stood on the red-velvet-covered riser and gazed inside the mouth of a burly, distressed miner and shook her head. She would have to remove the tooth that was causing the prospector so much pain. Nellie selected a corkscrew-type instrument to begin the process. She wrapped the tool around the tooth and with considerable effort wrenched it out of the man's mouth. The relief he felt was almost instantaneous.

Nellie Pooler Chapman was the first woman licensed to practice dentistry in the Old West. In her thirty-year career she would care for numerous residents in Nevada County, California. She was born in Norridgewock, Maine, in 1847 and at the age of thirteen relocated with her parents to the Gold Country. There she met and married Dr. Allen Chapman, a prominent dentist in the area. The parlor in the home he built for his new bride included a dental office.

Nellie did not enter the field of dentistry eagerly. She assisted her husband in his work but was not initially interested in the job as a career. It wasn't until she had spent years learning about the profession from Allen that she decided to apply for a license of her own. Nellie became a full-fledged dentist in 1879.

She was the first woman to be registered in the field in the western territories. When her husband decided to open an office in Virginia City, Nevada, Nellie chose to remain behind in California and continue working at the practice Allen had initially established. Allen traveled back and forth from his business in Nevada to visit his wife and children and help out at the busy Nevada City office. In his absence, Nellie was the sole dentist between Sacramento and Donner Lake.

Nellie Pooler Chapman, 1847–1906

SEARLS HISTORICAL LIBRARY

Dr. Chapman outfitted her thriving practice with a porcelain bowl, crystal water glasses, and the most modern drills and aspirators. The chair her patients sat in was covered in red velvet and labeled "Imperial Columbia" in gold script.

In 1897 Nellie's husband passed away. She continued on with the practice for another nine years, providing care for Northern California residents.

Nellie's talents extended well beyond dentistry. She was also an accomplished poet and a musician. She participated in the local

Shakespeare Club and wrote several musical compositions. In addition to her involvement in civic organizations, she was also a busy mother of two boys, both of whom followed their parents into the field of dentistry.

On April 7, 1906, Nellie Pooler Chapman passed away. Her sons donated the contents of her practice to the School of Dentistry in San Francisco. A glass cabinet contains some of her books, including an 1878 *Gray's Anatomy, Descriptive and Surgical,* an 1875 copy of *The Principles and Practice of Dental Surgery,* and other large leather-bound volumes containing technical and medical information.

Dr. Chapman was fifty-nine when she died and was buried at the Pioneer Cemetery in Nevada City, California.

The home where Nellie lived and worked still stands on the steep hillside above Deer Creek, a short distance from the location of the first gold strike in town. In spite of the fact that Nellie had solidified a place for women in the field of dentistry in the western territories, when she died the local newspaper, *The Daily Union,* barely recognized her professional achievements. The obituary lauded her other talents as a writer, composer, and elocutionist, and, in one line, mentioned that she had "practiced dentistry for many years in the city."

Charles Shibell

d. 1908

"The way I hear it . . . it was a dead square fight and that you couldn't tell who shot who first."

— CHARLES SHIBELL'S COMMENTS ABOUT
THE GUNFIGHT AT THE OK CORRAL, 1881

Charles A. Shibell was the sheriff of Pima County, Arizona, during the time one of the most famous events in the state, if not the West, took place—the gunfight at the OK Corral. His career in law enforcement began in 1874 when he was asked to serve as deputy undersheriff. In 1876 he became sheriff, overseeing the area from Tucson to Tombstone. Among the many men he appointed Arizona deputies were John Behan and Wyatt Earp.

He was born in St. Louis, Missouri, on August 14, 1841. He was an educated man who received good grades throughout school. After graduation he moved to California in search of gold. In 1860 he settled in Sacramento and worked as a clerk for a stage line. Unsatisfied with the sedentary position, Shibell took a job as a freight runner transporting goods from San Jose to Santa Fe.

In February 1862 he signed on as a teamster with the California Column of the United States Army. He traveled with the 1st and 5th California Infantry and the 1st California Cavalry

Charles Alexander Shibell, 1841–1908

Regiment. Along the way he helped fight off hostile Natives and highwaymen who were out to steal military payrolls.

Of the many locations Shibell visited, Tucson was his favorite. After he was honorably discharged from the army, he made the Southern Arizona town his home. Shibell became part owner of a stagecoach line that carried supplies back and forth along the treacherous route between the Old Pueblo and Yuma. His background dealing with Indians upset about wagons traipsing through their land was instrumental in negotiating a peaceful agreement to get the goods through safely.

In addition to his responsibilities as a mediator and business owner, Shibell was also a rancher and farmer. He had a talent for managing money and put it to work as the treasurer of not only the Tucson Building and Loan Association but the Citizens Builder and Consumer Association as well.

Not all of his endeavors were as civilized as banking and being a land baron. A raid by Apache Indians on a lumber camp in the Santa Rita Mountains near Tucson prompted Shibell to reenlist in the military in order to bring the natives to "justice."

The Apaches had kidnapped two girls when they overtook the Santa Rita settlement and were willing to release them only if some Apache prisoners were set free first. On April 30, 1871, Shibell and several other residents attacked the sleeping Indian camp and killed 118 men, women, and children. The two young women who were taken hostage were rescued, and one later married Charles Shibell.

Shibell ventured from Arizona only once and that was to take the job of customs inspector in El Paso, Texas. The bulk of his adult life was spent in Tucson. During Shibell's time as Pima County sheriff he led several posses in pursuit of outlaws and cattle rustlers. In 1878 he organized a team of six lawmen to track down a robber named William Brazzleton. After Brazzleton was brought to justice, Shibell had his body placed on display at the sheriff's office as a deterrent to other criminals.

Shibell took a step out of public service in 1882 and concentrated on a hotel business. He owned and operated two of

Arizona's most popular Old West hotels, the Occidental and the Palace.

He returned to public office in 1888, serving as Pima County recorder. He was elected to the post six times. He also served as undersheriff during the same period. Sheriff Shibell was married three times and had two children. He died on October 21, 1908, and was laid to rest at Evergreen City in the town he cherished— Tucson.

His funeral was attended by family members, several Native American friends from the Apache Indian Reservation outside of Tucson, and the governor of Arizona, Joseph Henry Kibbey. Kibbey praised Shibell's contributions to law and order in southern Arizona and credited him with helping to bring about peace between the Apache Indians and the white people in the territory.

Pat Garrett

d. 1908

"Pat, you son-of-a-bitch, they told me there was a
hundred Texans here from the Canadian River!
If I'd a-known there wasn't no more than this,
you'd never have got me!"

— BILLY THE KID TO PAT GARRETT IMMEDIATELY
AFTER STEPPING OUT OF THE ROCK HOUSE AT STINKING
SPRINGS AND SURRENDERING TO GARRETT'S POSSE

Patrick Floyd Jarvis Garrett is remembered best for being the man who shot Billy the Kid. But his contribution to taming the American West consisted of much more than that single event—for more than eighteen years, the lawman tracked down numerous outlaws running wild along the Texas-New Mexico border.

Garrett was born on June 5, 1850, in Chambers County, Alabama. When he was three years old, his parents, John and Elizabeth, purchased a plantation in Louisiana and moved their children to their new home near the town of Haynesville, Alabama. At the age of nineteen, the six-foot, four-inch Pat struck out on his own and made his way to the Texas Panhandle, where he signed on with a team of ranchers driving herds of cattle to market. Eventually he left that work to become a buffalo hunter.

The first gunfight Garrett was involved in occurred in

November 1876 in Fort Griffith, Texas, when a heated exchange with a buffalo skinner over some hides resulted in a fistfight and further escalated to gunplay. Garrett, who was an excellent marksman, shot the man in the chest.

Shortly after the incident he departed Texas and rode into New Mexico, where he became a cowpuncher for a Lincoln County rancher. During his employment as a ranch hand there, he met and married a young woman named Juanita Gutierrez, who died within a year after the wedding. He later married Juanita's sister Apolinana, and the couple had nine children.

In 1878 Garrett traded in his job as a cowboy to become a saloon owner. He catered to the rough range riders, serving not only drinks but food as well. When Garrett wasn't tending bar, he was gambling and dealing faro to his customers. Enter William H. Bonney, better known as Billy the Kid, a frequent patron. Pat and Billy got along very well together and became fast friends, swapping stories of the rough life on the frontier. Billy trusted Pat and regarded him as an older brother. Because both liked to gamble, the pair gave each other the nicknames of Little Casino and Big Casino. Garrett knew the Kid's hideouts and his partners in crime. It was in part Garrett's friendship with the Kid that prompted territory officials to appoint him to the post of sheriff. His background as a reformed gunfighter and his familiarity with the notorious outlaw made him a natural for the job.

Garrett was sworn in as the Lincoln County sheriff on November 7, 1880. The war between the cattle barons and Billy the Kid was in full swing. The Kid and his friends had shot and killed several of the gunmen hired by the cattle barons to kill the Kid's employer and mentor, John Tunstall. Garrett's job was to put an end to the conflict and arrest Billy and his cohorts.

The sheriff and his deputies took out after the fugitive and caught up with him in late December. The Kid was taken into

The Garrett family plot in Las Cruces, New Mexico

custody and escorted to the town of Mesilla to stand trial, where he was convicted on murder charges and sentenced to be hanged. But days before the punishment was to be enforced, the Kid escaped in a hail of gunfire.

Garrett formed another posse and, following a tip that the Kid was hiding with his friends at the army post, rode to Fort Sumner. On July 15, 1881, under the cover of darkness, Sheriff Garrett and his men snuck into the compound and surprised the Kid. Before the outlaw could draw his weapon, Garrett fired his own gun twice and killed him.

The news that Pat Garrett had brought down the notorious Billy the Kid spread quickly across the West and brought the key players in the shootout instant fame. Because of Pat's previous affiliation with the young renegade and the sympathy he had for

Billy's desperate situation, some historians question Garrett's account of the Kid's demise and maintain he escaped. The debate has kept people interested in the lawman and outlaw for decades.

Garrett finished his term as sheriff in 1882, and he then turned his attention to ranching and politics. In 1884 he made an unsuccessful run for the New Mexico state senate as well as a bid for the Republican nomination to serve another two years as sheriff. Garrett returned to Texas to work as a ranger and achieved the rank of captain in the corps.

From 1885 to 1896 the restless lawman traveled back and forth from New Mexico to Texas several times. He held various high-profile jobs in both places, including serving as county commissioner in Uvalde, Texas County, and sheriff of Dona Ana County, New Mexico. In 1901 President Theodore Roosevelt appointed him as customs inspector in El Paso. After holding the position for five years, he retired to his ranch in Las Cruces, New Mexico.

On February 29, 1908, Garrett was involved in a feud over land he had leased to a farmer. Garrett objected to the farmer's goats grazing on acreage he believed should be for cattle only. The minor range war sparked a deadly outcome. One of the men Garrett had argued with ambushed him and shot him in the back of the head when the famous ex-sheriff had stopped to relieve himself.

The former lawman's lifeless body was left on the side of the road until Las Cruces Sheriff Felipe Lucero arrived on the scene four hours later and identified the dead man. Garrett's tall frame would not fit in the average-size coffin of five-foot, five-inches, and a special casket had to be made for him. After his body was placed inside the coffin, his body was put on display at Strong's Undertaking Parlor.

Funeral services for Pat Garrett, held on March 5, 1908, were attended by hundreds of southern New Mexico residents. The graveside service included a eulogy from Garrett's longtime friend and well-known gambler, Tom Powers. Pat Garrett was laid to rest beside his daughter, Ida, at the Masonic Cemetery in Las Cruces, New Mexico.

The cemetery is located at 760 South Compress Road in Dona Ana County.

The cattleman who shot and killed Garrett later confessed to the murder. The judge who presided over the man's hearing had disliked Garrett because he felt he was arrogant. His bias prompted him to rule that the rancher had acted in self-defense, and the man was acquitted.

Red Cloud

d. 1909

"My sun is set. My day is done. Darkness is stealing over me. Before I lie down to rise no more, I will speak to my people."

— CHIEF RED CLOUD'S FINAL ADDRESS
TO THE LAKOTA TRIBE, 1909

A bitter blast of wind swept down the Platte River, and the watcher on the low bank took refuge under the projecting canopy of rocks. Thirteen-year-old Red Cloud sat atop his horse staring at the water coursing madly and swirling in black eddies ahead of the icy gale. He sat his mount with grace and ease; rider and horse appeared as one against the pristine Nebraska landscape. He imagined his father was looking over him from the great beyond, proud of the way his son carried himself.

Red Cloud's father had placed the boy on the back of a spirited colt when he was six years old and offered advice that would stick with him throughout his life. "My son," Red Cloud's father began. "When you are able to sit quietly upon the back of this colt without bridle or saddle, I shall be glad, for the boy who can win a wild creature and learn to use it will be as a man, able to win and rule men."

Chief Red Cloud,- Cayuga.
Copyright 1901 by C. D. Arnold.

Oglala Lakota Chief Red Cloud, 1822–1909

Red Cloud is considered by many Native Americans to be one of the most important Sioux Indian leaders of all time. His wisdom, courage, and strong eloquent manner of speaking helped negotiate treaties with the imposing white settlers.

Red Cloud was born in Nebraska in 1822. His mother, an Ogallala Indian, and his father, a Brule Red Cloud, named him Makhpiya-Lutta. Makhpiya's (or Red Cloud as he would later be known) father died before he was thirteen years old, leaving his mother's brother to become the leader of the family.

Red Cloud was an accomplished bow hunter and lariat thrower. His hunting skills served his tribe well when warring with the neighboring Crow, Shoshone, and Ute Indians. He was able to disarm his enemies not only with physical weapons but with his intellect as well. Red Cloud was commended by his people for his ability to exercise restraint when necessary and for his remarkable efforts in battle. By the time he was twenty-eight, he was recognized as a man who could bravely represent his people in all territorial disputes.

In the beginning the Sioux nation did not try to stop the insurgence of white men onto their ancestral home. They believed there was enough land to go around and were willing to make allowances for a few pioneers. It was only when the Native American's hunting grounds and the buffalo began to disappear that they fought to regain their territory.

Red Cloud was called upon by the leaders of his tribe to organize a war party to drive the white man back. In 1866 Red Cloud and a number of Sioux warriors, including Crazy Horse and Dull Knife, attacked the inhabitants at Fort Phil Kearney in Wyoming. They killed eight soldiers and established themselves as a serious threat to the U.S. Army.

A commission of politicians from the East was sent to discuss an end to the growing conflict between the Indians and the whites. Red Cloud would agree to peace only if all the army forts within

*Chief Red Cloud was highly respected by his people
and considered a patriot.*

the Lakota Sioux territory were abandoned. The U.S. government agreed and left the area. The Black Hills and the Bighorn were again solely Indian country.

The discovery of gold in the region prompted a new rush onto Sioux land in 1874, and the U.S. government did little to stop it. For a while, Red Cloud held his ground and, along with other tribes, battled the persistent miners and their military protection.

The army launched a flurry of attacks on the Sioux people in retaliation for the massacre at the battle at Little Bighorn. The Sioux were vastly outnumbered, and after a valiant stand, they were forced to yield to the U.S. demand that they be removed to a reservation.

Red Cloud and his people were taken to the Pine Ridge Reservation in South Dakota. Their actions were continually watched by U.S. troops who frequently withheld food and other supplies. Red Cloud asserted his considerable authority to try to make sure the government was held responsible for the promises they had broken to the Indians. With the help of a Yale University professor, an official investigation was launched to look into the United States' willingness to break the treaties they had signed with the Sioux. The case resulted in the dismissal of several corrupt key figures involved in Indian affairs.

Red Cloud reluctantly remained on the reservation for more than thirty years. He continued to resist being conquered by the white man and argued against leasing the land of his forefathers to the United States government and dividing the reservation into individual sections. Historians note that the Lakota leader was a quiet, dignified man who lost his eyesight in the last few years of his life. The eighty-seven-year-old man converted to Christianity before dying on December 10, 1909, and his simple, respectful funeral was attended by several family members and friends. He is buried at the Native American Cemetery in Shannon County, South Dakota.

Carrie Nation

d. 1911

"Men are nicotine-soaked, beer-besmirched, whiskey-greased, red-eyed devils."

—Carrie Nation, 1887

The barroom at the Hotel Carey in Wichita, Kansas, was extremely busy most nights. Cowhands and trail riders arrived by following the smell of whiskey and the sound of an inexperienced musician playing an out-of-tune piano inside the saloon. Beyond the swinging doors awaited a host of well-used female companions and an assortment of alcohol to help drown away the stresses of life on the rugged plains. Patrons were too busy drinking, playing cards, or flirting with soiled doves to notice the stout, six-foot-tall woman enter the saloon. She wore a long black alpaca dress and bonnet and carried a Bible. Almost as if she were offended by the obvious snub, the matronly newcomer loudly announced her presence. As it was December 23, 1900, she shouted, "Glory to God! Peace on earth and good will to men!"

At the conclusion of her proclamation, she hurled a massive brick at the expensive mirror hanging behind the bar and shattered the center of it. As the stunned bartender and customers looked on, she pulled an iron rod from under her full skirt and began tearing the place apart.

The sheriff was quickly sent for, and soon the violent woman was being escorted out of the business and marched to the local jail. As the door on her cell was slammed shut and locked, she yelled out to the men, "You put me in here a cub, but I will go out a roaring lion and make all hell howl."

Carrie Nation's tirade echoed throughout the Wild West. For decades the lives of women from Kansas to California had been adversely affected by their husbands', fathers', and brothers' abuse of alcohol. Carrie was one of the first to take such a public, albeit forceful, stance against the problem. The Bible-thumping, brick- and bat-wielding Nation was a member of the Women's Christian Temperance Union. The radical organization, founded in 1874, encouraged wives and mothers concerned about the effects of alcohol to join in the crusade against liquor and the sellers of vile drink. Beginning in 1899, prior to Carrie's outbursts, the group had primarily subscribed to peaceful protests.

Carrie had been born Carrie Amelia Moore on November 25, 1846, in Garrard County, Kentucky. Her father was an itinerate minister who moved his wife and children from Kentucky to Texas, then on to Missouri and back again to Kentucky. Carrie married in 1866. Her husband was a heavy drinker, and after their wedding she pleaded with him to stop. After six months of persistent nagging, Carrie's husband still refused to give up the bottle. With a child on the way, she left him and returned home. He died of acute alcoholism one month before the baby boy was born.

Not long after this death, Carrie remarried, but David Nation possessed the same love for alcohol. He was a lawyer and a minister who did not share in what he called "his wife's archaic view" about liquor. Their differences of opinion not only interfered with their personal life but wreaked havoc on David's professional life as well.

CARRIE NATION

Carrie Amelia Nation, 1846–1911

The Nations moved to Texas, and Carrie immediately joined the Methodist church. Her outlandish beliefs and revelations prompted the members of the congregation to dismiss her. Carrie then formed her own religious group and held weekly meetings at the town cemetery. In 1889 Carrie insisted that David move her and their children to Medicine Lodge, Kansas. Kansas had a prohibition law, and Carrie believed the fact that liquor was outlawed would stop David from partaking of any libations.

Determined Kansas residents found ways to drink and so did Reverend Nation. Drugstores and clubs sold whiskey in backrooms and alleys, calling the liquid medicine instead of alcohol. Carrie was outraged. Not only did she chastise members of her husband's assembly in Sunday service, but she also scolded those whom she knew drank when she saw them on the street.

Carrie believed the Lord had called her to take such drastic action against alcohol. According to her autobiography, *The Use and Need of the Life of Carrie Nation,* she felt it was her duty to defend the family home and fight for other women locked in marriages with excessive drinkers.

At the age of fifty-three, she marched into a drugstore on the main street of Medicine Lodge and preached the evils of drink to all the customers. She was tossed out of the business, but a crowd of women who had gathered to inquire about the excitement applauded her efforts. Their response and the Women's Christian Temperance Union members spurred her on. She continued to visit liquor stores until all the bars in town were effectively forced to close.

Carrie waged a one-woman campaign against saloons across Kansas and into Oklahoma. There were times she entered barrooms with a hatchet and smashed tables and bottles of beer. She was arrested on numerous occasions and spent several nights in jail. Her demonstrations made the front page of newspapers from Boston to

Independence. She was recognized as a heroine by women everywhere and hailed as a courageous fighter for the cause.

David Nation was unimpressed with his wife's devotion and tried to convince her to abandon the quest and settle down. She refused, sued for divorce, and turned to the lecture circuit as a way to support herself and her children. Her following was substantial, but when she took to appearing in vaudeville-style shows and selling souvenir hatchet pins, many of her supporters turned against her. The Women's Christian Temperance Union had a change of heart about her, as well, and withdrew their endorsement of her.

The last public assault Carrie waged on a tavern occurred in Butte, Montana, in January 1910. Her hatchet was poised to do damage, but the owner of the business, a woman named May Maloy, stopped her before she could strike a blow. Not long after the humiliating incident, Carrie retired from hatchet marching and dedicated her time strictly to speaking engagements.

She passed away on June 9, 1911, after collapsing during a speech at a park in Eureka Springs, Arkansas, at age sixty-five. Although her methods were considered extreme and unpopular by saloon owners and consumers of alcohol alike (one bar owner hung a sign on the front door of his establishment that read ALL NATIONS ACCEPTED EXCEPT CARRIE), her ideas about public reform did not go unnoticed by government officials. Her unconventional stance on drinking helped lay the groundwork for the passage of the Eighteenth Amendment, which banned "intoxicating liquors." The controversial bill was ratified in 1919, nine years after Carrie's death.

In her memoirs, published in 1905, the determined prohibitionist predicted that her anti-alcohol campaign would "eventually bear fruit." In Carrie's words, "this movement will help carry a nation."

Fiery Prohibitionist Carrie Nation died in June 1911.

Carrie Nation was buried at the Belton City Cemetery in Belton, Missouri, a location where she had spent a great deal of time in the final days of her life. Dual funeral services were held in Kansas City, Missouri, and Eureka Springs, Arkansas, for mourners who wanted to pay tribute to her memory. The tombstone over Carrie's grave, erected by the Women's Christian Temperance Union in 1924, reads FAITHFUL TO THE CAUSE OF PROHIBITION, SHE HATH DONE WHAT SHE COULD.

Rosa May

d. 1911

"I hope business is good with you, darling and that you are happy. If you'll believe me I'll think the world of little Rose."

— THE CONTENTS OF A NOTE FROM ONE OF ROSA MAY'S CUSTOMERS IDENTIFIED ONLY AS JACK, DECEMBER 12, 1876

Several hundred yards away from the weather-worn fence surrounding the Odd Fellows Cemetery in Bodie, California, a single tombstone stands alone in the brush. The crude markings on the rock grave are of a cross and the name of the person buried underneath. There are no dates or sentimental verses etched on the stone. It simply reads ROSA MAY.

Rosa May was a prostitute who moved to the wild, gold-mining camp of Bodie in 1891. The thirty-year-old "sporting woman" was born in Pennsylvania. She came west at the age of twenty with the hope of making a fortune off the gold and silver miners. Prostitution was the single largest occupation for women beyond the Mississippi River, and Rosa May was a success in that line of work. She settled first in Virginia City, Nevada, but had a business in Carson City, Nevada, as well.

Although she had regular customers in every location she

worked, her heart belonged to bartender Erni Marks. She followed her lover to Bodie, where he served drinks at a saloon owned by his brother. Erni would not call on Rosa May during the day for fear of soiling his reputation, nor would he openly admit an association with the petite beauty.

While he adamantly denied having a relationship with Rosa May to his family and friends, behind closed doors he professed his love to her. She returned the sentiment and dreamed of the day they could leave the area and marry. But both Erni and Rosa May struggled with various debilitating illnesses that shortened their life expectancies. Rosa frequently suffered from chills and fever, a condition that originated when she lived in the cold, flimsy parlor houses in the East. Erni was hampered with gout and had contracted a venereal disease.

Rosa May, 1854–1911

COURTESY MONO COUNTY DEPARTMENT OF PARKS AND RECREATION AND BODIE STATE HISTORICAL PARK

Erni promised to handle her funeral arrangements and see to it a monument was erected at her gravesite if Rosa May were to die before him. In 1911 Rosa contracted pneumonia and died at the age of fifty-seven. Erni's always bleak financial situation prevented him from purchasing the headstone he assured Rosa he would buy. What's more, attempts to have her buried within the cemetery were thwarted. Prostitutes were not allowed to be "laid to rest"

Sporting women, or soiled doves, as they were also known,
were not allowed to be buried with the "respectable" Bodie citizens.

alongside members of "polite society." Erni was forced to inter Rosa May in what was referred to as the "outcast cemetery." A wooden cross marked the spot.

Erni continued to work at the bar until 1919, when Prohibition drove him out of the saloon business. Relatives back East supported him until his death in 1928.

Legend has it that he asked to be buried next to his "little girl," Rosa, but he was buried in the Odd Fellows Cemetery, far away from the outcast graveyard located in the Basin Range, east of the Sierra Nevada, thirteen miles east of U.S. Highway 395 in central California.

In death as in life, Erni was publicly distant from Rosa May.

Stagecoach Mary

d. 1914

*"God pours life into death and death into life without a
drop being spilled."*

—AUTHOR UNKNOWN

A well-traveled trail rests peacefully between the rich forested hill-
sides around the town of Cascade, Montana, and snakes seventeen
miles west to St. Peter's Mission. The road, as well as the mission
itself, was the hub of activity in 1895. Back and forth along the
route, Mary Fields, a former slave from Tennessee, drove a stagecoach carrying mail for people in the central area of the state. Mary
was the first African American to deliver the mail and the oldest
woman to ever take on such a job.

Fields was born in 1832 and lived with her parents on the
Dunn Plantation in Hickman County, Tennessee. Shortly after the
Civil War ended, Mary became a free woman. At the urging of her
good friend Dolly Dunn, Mary headed west to Montana. Dolly
had become a nun and founded a boarding school for Native
Americans called St. Peter's Mission. She invited Mary to visit and
consider staying on if she liked.

Once the tough, six-foot-tall Fields arrived, she discovered
the mission to be in a state of disrepair. She organized a team of

Mary Fields, 1832–1914

men to work on the school and make repairs and improvements. One of the workers resented a black woman telling him what to do and in a fit of rage backhanded her across the mouth. Just as he was going for his gun, Mary pulled her own six-shooters out first and shot and killed him. The altercation led to her being asked to leave the mission.

Mary then applied for work as a mail carrier on a new route opening into the Cascade Mountains. After proving she could defend herself and her cargo from highwaymen and demonstrating her talent with horses and driving a stage, she was offered the job. She was sixty years old.

Stagecoach Mary, as she would come to be known, transported letters and packages to and from pioneers for five years. She left the United States Mail Service in 1900 and opened a laundry business in Cascade. The business was a huge success, and she spent a portion of the profits treating herself to whiskey and cigars at a local saloon.

Mary Fields is recognized by the United States Postal Service as being the second woman in history to drive the mail across the Western frontier. She and her mule "Moses" delivered important correspondence that helped to advance the land-claim process and bring about the development of a considerable portion of central Montana.

Sometimes referred to as "Black Mary," Fields proved a woman could do anything a man could do in the untamed territories beyond the Rockies. Among her many admirers were actor Gary Cooper, who knew her when he was a little boy growing up in her neighborhood in Cascade, and sculptor, illustrator, and painter Charles M. Russell. Russell made a pen-and-ink drawing of the pioneer in 1897. The image, entitled "A Quiet Day in Cascade," features Mary being knocked down by a hog and spilling a basket of eggs.

Mary Fields was a proud, independent woman who never wanted to be an inconvenience to her friends and neighbors. When she became seriously ill in 1914, she snuck off to a tall, grassy area outside her home and lay down to die. Children playing in the area found her and she was taken to the Columbus Hospital in Great Falls, where she died of liver failure shortly after being admitted. The numerous townspeople she had befriended over time escorted her casket to the graveyard.

She was eighty-two years old when she passed away. A simple wooden cross marks the place where she was buried. Friends and admirers laid her to rest at the Hillside Cemetery near Cascade, Montana, located at the foot of the trail that leads the way to St. Peter's Mission.

Thomas Jonathan Jeffords

d. 1914

*"I found him to be a man of great natural ability, a
splendid specimen of physical manhood."*

— THOMAS JEFFORDS'S DESCRIPTION OF
APACE INDIAN CHIEF COCHISE, 1873

The wind howled through the massive rock monuments of the
Chiricahua mountain range near Tombstone, Arizona, like troops
of demons on their way to war. A tall man with sloping shoulders
walked with great purpose into the imposing scene. His granitelike
visage was partly hidden by an iron-gray mustache that curled
around to meet his thick sideburns. As he glanced about, the heads
of several Apache Indian warriors emerged, and they eyed the daring traveler as he proceeded into the labyrinth of stone and cactus.

Cochise, the leader of the Chiricahua Apaches, slowly
appeared on the path where the man was walking. Behind the chief
stood several armed braves. The man nodded to Cochise and
introduced himself as Thomas Jonathan Jeffords. "I'm here to
speak with you personally," Jeffords explained in broken Apache.

Impressed with his boldness and attempt to speak the Apache
language, Cochise welcomed teamster Thomas Jeffords into his
camp. The two men talked about the wagon pass that ran through

Thomas Jonathan Jeffords

Apache land. Several teamsters hauling supplies to southern Arizona settlements had been killed by Cochise's men. Jeffords operated the stage line, and fourteen of the twenty-one drivers the Apaches had gunned down had worked for him. His goal was to convince Cochise to allow his wagons to go through without assault. The meeting proved to be a success in more ways than one. Not only did Cochise agree to stop the raids on Jeffords's supply line, but the two became lifelong friends. "He respected me and I respected him," Jeffords wrote in his journal in 1878. "He was a man who scorned a liar. He was truthful in all things. His religion was truth and loyalty."

Cochise's acceptance of Jeffords led the Chiricahua tribe to approve of the frontiersman. They called him Tyazalaton, which meant sandy whiskers. Cochise gave him the name Chicksaw, or brother.

Jeffords was born on January 1, 1832, in Chautauqua, New York—a long way from the western landscape he would eventually call home. His formative years were spent piloting steamboats up and down the Mississippi River. In 1859 he traveled across the plains to the New Mexico Territory to work as an army scout. He pursued hostile Natives bent on killing white invaders on their land. Jeffords was also an excellent hunter and road builder as well.

A skirmish between white settlers and the Apaches over an unauthorized trail through Native land ended in the Indians' withdrawal from the area. The withdrawal was only temporary, however, and a war ensued. Jeffords participated in the Battle of Apache Pass and helped establish a military post to protect pioneers from being ambushed by the Indians. Once the post was completed, Jeffords turned his attention to being a teamster. He hauled food, meat, and mail over the wild terrain along the Rio Grande, from Mesilla, New Mexico, to Tucson, Arizona.

When the situation between the Apache Indians and the U.S. government erupted into the Cochise war in 1871, again because of uninvited settlers on Native American soil, Jeffords was called upon to help. Fort Bowie's commander, General Oliver Howard, was aware Jeffords was friends with Cochise and asked him to arrange a meeting with Cochise to talk peace. Jeffords agreed and his efforts resulted in a treaty being drawn up between the United States and the Chiricahua Indians.

The terms Cochise agreed to included a provision that all the Chiricahua Apaches had to be moved to a reservation. Cochise consented only after Jeffords was named Indian agent for the Apaches. Jeffords held the post for four years until 1876, two years after Cochise died, he was released from his duties. He went on to serve as a scout for the army and helped with the apprehension of Geronimo.

Thomas Jonathan Jeffords died on February 19, 1914, at a mining camp outside of Tucson, Arizona. His twilight years had

ARIZONA HISTORICAL CENTER/TUCSON, #28494

The frontiersman, scout, and Indian agent is buried
at Evergreen Cemetary in Tucson, Arizona.

been spent prospecting for gold in the Tortolita Mountains. He was eighty-two when he passed away from natural causes and was laid to rest at the Evergreen Cemetery in Tucson.

Jeffords's funeral was attended by local government officials and hundreds of Apache Indians. The headboard over his grave reads FRIEND AND BLOOD-BROTHER OF COCHISE. PEACE-MAKER WITH HOSTILE APACHES. Descendants of Cochise who still reside in the area continue to honor the memory of the individual history records as "the only white man the leader ever trusted" by placing a wreath of white flowers on Jeffords's grave once a month.

Jeffords's part in helping to bring about peace between the ever encroaching white settlers and the warring Apache Indians was so significant that noted historian Dee Brown immortalized Jeffords's role in the book *Bury My Heart at Wounded Knee.*

Buffalo Bill Cody

d. 1917

"Wanted—young, skinny, wiry fellows not over 18. Must be expert riders willing to risk death daily. Orphans preferred."

— Newspaper advertisement Cody responded to in order to become a courier for the Pony Express, 1860

Buffalo Bill Cody is credited with bringing the adventures of taming America's Wild West to the world. Using a talented cast of cowboys, cowgirls, Indians, and trick ropers and riders, the ambitious entertainer created a show that re-created life on the frontier. Among the long list of Western legends who performed in Cody's program were Wild Bill Hickok, Chief Sitting Bull, and Annie Oakley.

William Frederick Cody was born in Iowa on February 26, 1846. His parents moved to Kansas when he was eight years old. His father passed away when Cody was eleven, and the youngster helped support the family by working as an ox-team driver and a messenger for a company that would later create the Pony Express. He never cared much for school and dropped out in 1859, choosing instead to venture west.

Cody held a variety of jobs on his way to becoming famous

on several continents. He was an army scout, soldier, gold prospector, teamster, trapper, and hunter. He earned his moniker, Buffalo Bill, hunting buffalo to feed the Transcontinental Railroad construction crews. He met Louisa Frederici in St. Louis in 1864, and the two married shortly thereafter.

When the Unites States government wanted to expand the country's borders in late 1860, they recruited seasoned plainsmen like Cody to help them in their quest. Buffalo Bill proved to be an invaluable asset in dealing with Natives who were hostile about the invasion of their land. In 1872 he was awarded the Congressional Medal of Honor for his efforts fighting the Indians along the Platte River. Newspaper accounts of his acts of bravery helped make his name a household word.

Cody's idea for a Wild West show was conceived with the help of writer Ned Buntline. Buntline had transformed the highlights of Cody's frontier experience into several best-selling books. The pair decided to parlay that success into a stage show, and in December 1872 they presented their first program, entitled "Scouts of the Plains." The show was an instant hit with audiences from Boston to Topeka.

After working with Buntline for several years, Cody decided to form his own company. Together with friends and fellow scout Texas Jack Omohundro and his press agent and manager, John M. Burke, the Wild West Circus tour was born.

From 1883 to 1886 the Wild West show grew into a grand spectacle. It featured musicians, animal acts, rifle marksmen, and reenactments of such momentous events as the Battle of Little Bighorn and the holdup of the Deadwood Stage.

Buffalo Bill took his show abroad in 1887, performing for the queen of England, the Prince of Wales, and the czar of Russia. The action-packed performances attracted fans by the thousands. Audiences were not only entertained but also educated about the

BUFFALO BILL MUSEUM AND GRAVE, GOLDEN, COLORADO

The western frontiersman and entertainer Buffalo Bill Cody died during a visit to Denver in 1917.

customs of the American Indian and the life of Western settlers. Cody's show ran for thirty years and made millions in the process. Due to more than a few unwise business investments, he lost millions as well.

Buffalo Bill died on January 10, 1917, at age seventy-four, after suffering for two months with kidney failure. Although his will, drafted by Cody several years before his death, specified he was to be buried in Cody, Wyoming, his family laid him to rest atop Lookout Mountain in Colorado. According to his children their father had asked them to bury him at that location before he passed away.

The road to the site was snow–covered, and it was six months before Cody's grave could be dug. His embalmed remains were transported to the area on June 2, 1917, and his funeral was held the next day. More than twenty-thousand mourners attended the "open casket" service. Letters of condolence from Cody's friends, President Woodrow Wilson, and Chief Jack Red Cloud were sent to his grieving family.

Weeks after the funeral rumors began circulating that some of Cody's relatives, upset about where he was buried, were threatening to move his body to Wyoming. The troubling and persistent gossip prompted the Colorado National Guard to place a World War I tank on Lookout Mountain to protect Cody's remains from being disturbed. When Buffalo Bill's wife died in 1921, two tons of cement were poured over the site to secure their resting place.

Lookout Mountain is located west of Denver between Denver and Golden, Colorado. Millions have visited the massive tombstone that stands over the Old West celebrity's grave.

Bat Masterson
d. 1921

"There are many in this old world of ours who hold that things break about even for all of us. I have observed, for example, that we all get the same amount of ice. The rich get it in the summertime and the poor get it in the winter."

—BAT MASTERSON, 1906

Legendary lawmen William Barclay Masterson had a reputation for being a tough talker, an excellent shot, and a dandy dresser. He wore tailor-made suits and a derby hat and carried a gold-headed cane. He was a handsome, well-liked character with black hair and blue eyes who was extremely fast on the draw.

Born in Illinois on November 22, 1855, Bat (as he was more commonly known) was the second of five brothers. His parents were homesteaders who moved their family to a prairie farm in Wichita, Kansas, in 1871. At the age of nineteen, Bat persuaded two of his brothers to abandon farm life for a job hunting buffalo. The Masterson boys stuck together for a while, but the trio split up when his siblings decided to return home and Bat decided to continue on with the difficult work.

For more than a year, Bat roamed from Topeka to the Texas

William Barclay Masterson, 1855–1921

Panhandle. He changed employment often: He was a section hand for the Santa Fe Railroad, a ranch hand, and an Indian scout for the army. After his first gunfight in January 1876, in which Bat killed a man who fired on him and the woman he was with, he headed for Dodge City. There he invested in the Lone Star Dance Hall on the main street of town, and the establishment proved to be profitable.

Not long after Bat's arrival in the rough-and-tumble town, he helped a prisoner escape from jail. He'd had too much to drink and involved himself in an arrest that had nothing to do with him. The town marshal gave Bat a beating that turned him around so much so Masterson decided he would never go against the law again. In fact, the incident opened his eyes to the possibility of a future as an officer of the law.

Bat followed his brothers—one a marshal, the other a deputy—into the field of law enforcement. Bat campaigned hard for the position of Ford County sheriff deputy and was subsequently awarded the job. He was an effective lawman who tried to talk perpetrators into surrendering rather than resorting to gunplay. Using his fists and finesse, he persuaded many wrongdoers to "leave town peacefully" or "be carried out with a bullet hole in their chest."

Bat had an impressive and famous array of friends that included Wyatt Earp and Doc Holliday. Outlaws who knew of their association refused to tangle with Masterson for fear the Earp brothers and Holliday would come after them.

Before Bat's siblings were killed in the line of duty, the men participated in numerous posses that successfully tracked down and apprehended outlaws in the area. As such, the plains around Ford County during Masterson's time in office were relatively peaceful.

A controversial act drove Bat out of law enforcement in April

1881. Bat was in Tombstone, Arizona, when he got the news that one of his brother's lives was being threatened by a ruthless businessman. He quickly made his way back to Dodge City and arrived just in time to face the bad guys on the street. Once the smoke cleared from the gun battle, Bat alone was left standing.

He resigned from his position as an officer and left Kansas to see the West. He traveled through New Mexico, Utah, and Texas, earning his keep at each location by gambling. His natural gift for storytelling led to a job writing newspaper articles in Crede, Colorado, where his work was noticed by a correspondent for the *New York Sun* who helped him secure a position as a sportswriter for the *New York Morning Telegraph* in 1901.

Bat returned to law enforcement in 1905 when President Theodore Roosevelt appointed the fifty-year-old man as a special United States marshal to the Oklahoma Territory. He did not hold the post long due to the prior commitment he had with the *Morning Telegraph*.

Just before noon on October 25, 1921, Bat headed up 8th Avenue from his New York apartment to the newspaper office and wrote his column for the next day. He died of a heart attack fifteen minutes after he finished writing the article. He was found slumped over his desk with his pen in one hand and his column in the other. He was laid to rest at the Woodlawn Cemetery in New York. The tombstone over his grave carries his name, date of birth, and the words LOVED BY EVERYONE.

Lillian Russell

d. 1922

"If a woman gets the reputation of being a professional beauty, it is hard work to live up to it."
—LILLIAN RUSSELL, THE THEATRE MAGAZINE, 1905

Old West entertainer Lillian Russell had the kind of beauty that stopped traffic from her earliest years. And she had a magnificent voice her mother paid to have trained when the young woman was in her teens. Born on December 4, 1861, in Clinton, Iowa, Lillian Russell (her birth name was Helen Louise Leonard) was educated at the Convent of the Sacred Heart in Chicago and attended finishing school at Park Institute. She took singing lessons and sang in the church choir at the Episcopal Church.

Lillian honed her singing and acting skills performing in a series of light operatic productions. Her mother felt the work was beneath her daughter's ability: She was convinced her child would never achieve worldwide success in such common shows as HMS. *Pinafore*. Lillian disagreed and set out to prove her mother wrong.

Before the svelte performer rose to the ranks of the "Frontier's Most Popular Attractions," Lillian decided to marry, settle into domestic life, and take on the role of mother and wife. It was a role her close friends said she was born to play.

In early 1880 she gave birth to a son. Although she was content to stay home with her children, theater owners persuaded her to return to the stage. A nurse was hired to care for the baby during performances and rehearsals—a decision Lillian regretted for the rest of her life. She returned from rehearsal one day to find her baby desperately ill. Despite all attempts to cure the infant, he died in convulsions. Apparently the inexperienced nurse had accidentally pierced his abdomen with a diaper pin. Her husband accused Lillian of neglect.

Grieving over the death of her son and feeling betrayed by her husband's accusations, Lillian concentrated on her career. Tony Pastor, legendary producer of musical comedy, heard her sing at the home of a friend and consequently offered her a job. At age nineteen, with a statuesque figure, golden curls, skin like "roses and cream," and a soprano voice that could do everything with ease, she had found her first mentor in Pastor.

The first thing Pastor did was to change his ingénue's name from Helen Louise Leonard to Lillian Russell. In 1880 he introduced her to East Coast audiences as "Lillian Russell, the English Ballad Singer." He was a brilliant manager, securing parts for her that showed off her talent.

She was a rousing success, so much so that Pastor feared she would be spoiled by the adulation. Instead of continuing to build her reputation in New York, he sent her west with Willie Edouin's touring company. As she traveled by rail toward the Pacific Ocean, she learned to play poker and pinochle.

In San Francisco Lillian Russell became the toast of the town. The City by the Bay was bubbling over with brash enterprise, fueled by newly made fortunes dug from the golden hills. The troupe earned recognition in the newspapers, and reporters took note of the fresh young singer who made several appearances. But despite the glowing reviews for Lillian, the acting troupe lost money and had to disband. Lillian returned to New York in the fall of 1881 and accepted an offer to play at the New York Bijou Opera House. From the Bijou she was summoned to England to perform at London's Gaiety Theatre. Her debut there set her star ablaze.

Shortly after she arrived in London, she met and fell in love with a musician and composer by the name of Edward Solomon. She and her first husband had divorced after the death of their baby, and even though she was surrounded by adoring fans, she was lonely. Solomon and Russell married in May 1884.

For a brief time Mr. and Mrs. Solomon were happy. By February 1885, the two had become parents of a little girl they named Dorothy. Then a woman who claimed to also be married to Edward filed suit against the composer for bigamy. Lillian's husband was arrested, and she quickly had their marriage annulled.

In 1886 Lillian returned to New York. After a brief stay she decided to make another tour across country, and this one turned out to be much more successful. She signed with the J. C. Duff Company and embarked on a long tour of cities along the Pacific Coast. At the end of the two seasons on the road, Lillian was a bigger star than ever. And, as she entered her thirties, she, herself, was bigger than ever. The hourglass figure that had contributed to her fame now required the tight cinching of a strong corset. Lillian, who reportedly could eat a dozen ears of corn as an appetizer, fully enjoyed the offerings of the best restaurants. Knowing her beauty was a huge part of her success, she began to exercise religiously. She became a fanatical bicyclist, and her friend, millionaire railroad salesman Diamond Jim Brady, presented her with a gold-plated bicycle.

As Lillian made her way across the West in her Pullman car, she met numerous admirers, such as tenor John Chatterton. The pair married in 1894, but the relationship didn't last. After her third failed marriage, she once again threw herself into her career

Lillian Russell, 1861–1923

and took over as manager of her own theater troupe.

The year 1912 was a year of change for Lillian Russell. After a great deal of thought and consideration, she retired from the stage and decided to pursue a career in writing and lecturing. She penned a national newspaper column advocating women's rights and traveled around the country sharing her philosophy of self-help with eager female audiences. Lillian also married for a fourth time. Her new husband, Alexander Penn Moore, was the self-assured publisher of the *Pittsburgh Leader* newspaper, and he was not intimidated by Lillian's success.

Moore encouraged his wife's own interest in politics, and Russell ultimately devoted much of her time to opening the Progressive Party headquarters in Pittsburgh. Taking that support, (Theodore Roosevelt, who was friends with the famed actress and her husband, founded the Progressive Party.) Lillian used her fame and influence to help sell Liberty Bonds during World War I and campaigned for the 1920 presidential candidate Warren Harding. After he was elected, he used the multitalented actress for special intelligence-gathering assignments in Europe.

On June 6, 1922, Lillian Russell passed away at the age of sixty-one. She had just completed a fact-finding mission for President Harding. The cause of death was listed as "cardiac exhaustion." The famous thespian was laid to rest in a solid silver casket. In honor of her passing and in commemoration for her contribution to the arts, theaters across the United States observed a moment of silence on the day of her funeral. Lillian was buried with full military honors at the Allegheny Cemetery in Pittsburgh, Pennsylvania.

The Allegheny Cemetery is the sixth-oldest rural graveyard in the United States. Visitors to the historic grounds stop by Lillian Russell's mausoleum regularly. In 1923 actress Mae West was one of the faithful followers who visited Lillian's burial site.

Lotta Crabtree

d. 1924

"Our backyard cornered on one facing street where the immortal Lotta lived. I was only 13, but for her I felt it a duty to gather the prettiest rose in the neighborhood every day. I'd wrap it up carefully and throw it into her backyard after dark. I would see the Fairy Star the following morning, fondling the flower in recognition, and all this time we talked only with our eyes."
—J. H. P. GEDGE, 1860

A little redheaded girl dressed as a leprechaun marched past a group of muddy miners into the center of their rustic camp. Her mother helped her onto a stump while a banjo player strummed a tune for the child, who soon began dancing an Irish jig. The delighted forty-niners clapped and cheered the girl on, and she laughed at their enthusiasm. After she finished entertaining the men, they tossed gold nuggets and coins at her feet. She beamed with pride at the applause, and her mother collected her earnings and tucked them inside a leather grip. One of the youngest entertainers to travel through the Sierra Mountains in the 1800s, Lotta Crabtree had diverse talents and an infectious laugh that made her

Charlotte Mignon Crabtree, 1847–1924

a star in the Gold Country, as well as the primary breadwinner for her family.

Lotta was born in New York in 1847 and given the name Charlotte Mignon Crabtree. Her father, John, moved his daughter and wife, Mary Ann, west in 1852. He was an unsuccessful business owner turned prospector who never found any gold. Lotta's mother was a strong woman who quickly assumed responsibility for her only child's well-being. Mary Ann worked odd jobs to support Lotta and paid for the child's training in theater and dance. She recognized the talent her daughter had and saw the opportunity to develop it at their temporary home in San Francisco.

Theatrical shows were very popular in San Francisco. The various playhouses were always filled with bored miners looking to be amused. As the need for entertainment grew, more performers came to town daily. Variety shows sprung up overnight and featured acrobats, singers, and slapstick comedians. Child actors were held in particularly high regard because they reminded the miners of the sons and daughters they had left behind to search for gold.

The Crabtrees moved to the mining community of Grass Valley, California, in 1853. Mary Ann reasoned that Lotta would be able to earn a substantial amount entertaining the lonely miners who were working claims around the rich foothills. Mary Ann enrolled Lotta in the only dance school in Grass Valley. The classes were conducted in the annex of a tavern, and many of the prospectors who stopped in the saloon for a drink gathered around to watch Lotta twirl across the tiny stage. Tears would well up in their eyes as they thought of their own children, and they would shower the tot with chunks of gold and other gifts of appreciation.

Lotta's natural talent and beauty attracted not only the attention of the miners but that of the notorious Lola Montez as well. She thought the child had great potential. Lola lived a few doors

Lotta Crabtree was known as America's lovable comedienne.
She died at the age of seventy-seven.

down from the Crabtrees' home, and she spent many hours teaching Lotta some of her dance steps and how to ride a horse. She adored Lotta and let her play in her costumes and dance to her German music box. She pleaded with Mary Ann to let her take the energetic child to Australia with her to tour the country. Mary Ann, who was expecting another child at the time, refused. She was, however, encouraged by Lola's interest in Lotta. She enrolled Lotta in more dance classes and added singing classes to her studies. By the age of ten, Lotta was one of the most talented children in the Gold Country. She had a wonderful voice, possessed a great sense of comic timing, and was a master of such dances as the fandango and the Highland fling.

In an effort to capitalize on her daughter's abilities, Mary Ann decided to join forces with a gentleman who managed a saloon where traveling players often appeared. The two put together their own company of musicians and actors and set off to tour the mining camps with their pint-size gold mine. Lotta was well received wherever the troupe went, and she earned thirteen dollars a night dancing and singing. After a few months and hundreds of dollars later, Mary Ann was convinced that Lotta's act could earn more money in big-city theaters. She then moved her daughter back to San Francisco.

Lotta performed at variety halls and amusement parks and soon became known as the "San Francisco Favorite." She was twelve years old and the sole support of her family, which now included two brothers.

Lotta Crabtree was a popular star and in constant demand. By 1863 she was earning more than forty-two thousand dollars a year. Mary Ann was a smart businesswoman and invested her daughter's money in real estate. She walked the streets of the towns Lotta performed in and bought up vacant lots she believed would be highly sought after as the town grew. Lotta had no head for finances and counted on her mother to pay all her bills and support her act.

In 1871 Lotta decided to take a break from performing and travel to Europe. While abroad she learned to paint, studied French, and took piano lessons. She drew attention everywhere she went. She would dress in white muslin and blue ribbons and drive a pony cart up and down the streets admiring the scenery.

She returned to America and the theater in 1875 and continued portraying children and younger parts in comical performances. She loved making people laugh and is considered by most historians as one of the theater's first comediennes. Lotta loved animals, and when she finally returned to her beloved San

Francisco to perform in yet another play, she purchased a fountain at the intersection of Kearney and Market Streets and donated it to the city so thirsty horses would have a place to get a drink.

Lotta retired from the theater at the age of forty-five. She was tired and wanted a chance to rest and enjoy the money she had made. When her mother died in 1909, she was beside herself with grief. She moved to Boston, where she lived a quiet, almost reclusive life. The remaining years of her life were spent painting and giving her money away.

Lotta Crabtree died of arteriosclerosis in 1924 at the age of seventy-seven. She left her estate, estimated at four million dollars, to veterans, animals, students of music and agriculture, needy children at Christmastime, and needy actors. She was buried next to her mother in Woodlawn Cemetery in New York City.

Nellie Cashman

d. 1925

*"I have mushed with men, slept out in the open, washed
with them and been with them constantly, and I have
never been offered an insult..."*

—Nellie Cashman, 1905

Ellen Cashman is recognized by historians as one of the most generous and wealthy individuals in the history of America's Old West. Lured across the continent by the news of the discovery of gold, Ellen, or Nellie as she was more commonly known, came looking for a fortune and found a higher purpose.

She was born in County Cork, Ireland, around 1850; the actual date is unknown. Her parents were struggling farmers devastated by failed potato crops. In addition to the financial strife, the Irish-Catholics were being persecuted by the British rule of the country. The bleak situation contributed to the death of Nellie's father, and left with two children and no viable means of support to raise them, Mrs. Cashman set sail to America with her daughters. She had heard job opportunities in America abounded and that food was readily available for everyone. When the three arrived in Boston, they found the city overcrowded with immi-

ARIZONA HISTORICAL SOCIETY/TUCSON #83

Nellie Cashman, "The Angel of Tombstone," 1850–1925

grants. Competition for work was fierce, but life in Boston was an improvement over their previous circumstances.

When Nellie was old enough to be employed, she was hired as a bellhop at a posh Boston hotel. One of the many hotel guests she met and conversed with was Ulysses S. Grant. Grant was impressed by her ambition and encouraged her to "go west" where young women were needed to help settle the wild frontier. It was a suggestion she took to heart and vowed to do one day. Over the next few years, she saved her money for the trip, and in 1869 Nellie and her sister and mother boarded the Transcontinental Railroad bound for San Francisco. Her ultimate destination was anywhere there were rich mining camps.

Nellie first traveled to Virginia City, Nevada, where silver and gold finds were making multimillionaires out of prospectors. She found work as a cook, and the grateful argonauts paid handsomely for her meals. In 1872 she used the income to purchase a boardinghouse.

When news of a rich find in northern British Columbia reached Nellie's ears in 1879, she packed her things and left Nevada. Once she reached the diggings along Dease Lake, she bought another boardinghouse and a restaurant.

Nellie had a head for business and a heart for the hurting and needy. She consistently offered help to down-on-their-luck miners, orphans, and widows. She organized a rescue mission for prospectors trapped in the snow and gave out free food and clothes. Her selfless giving earned her the nickname the "Miner's Angel."

In the fall of 1878, she relocated to Arizona where she started another successful restaurant in Tucson before making her way to the booming silver town of Tombstone. Nellie established two businesses in Tombstone, a boot and shoe store and a grocery store. The venture thrived and the entrepreneur used a portion of the profits to build churches and support hospitals. She was civic minded and never without a cause to back or a charity for which to raise funds.

For a while Nellie was content to stay in Arizona. Her sister and her sister's five children were now living in Tombstone.

Nellie divided her time between her family and her new business pursuits, a cafe and a boardinghouse. By 1883, however,

Nellie was on the move again, this time to Baja, California. Reports of the rich placer goldfields prompted her to visit the area. When the trip proved to be unprofitable, she returned to the Southwest. Tragedy struck Nellie's world in early 1884 when her widowed sister died of tuberculosis.

Nellie was left to raise her nieces and nephews, a responsibility she cherished. The task was daunting, but it did not keep her from her charity work or efforts to civilize the territory. She was against public hangings and fought tirelessly to stop local government from making them a form of entertainment.

From 1885 to 1897 Nellie bounced from one boomtown to another, buying and selling businesses and building a substantial bank account. On July 17, 1897 Nellie joined the Klondike gold rush and traveled to Dawson City, Alaska. She grubstaked a handful of miners and opened a cafe and supply store. She made a fortune selling supplies to eager prospectors. She never turned away a miner who didn't have money. She made sure they were cared for regardless of their means.

Nellie lived in the cold Yukon Territory for seven years. During that time she worked isolated mines with her nephew, driving her team of sled dogs from one claim to another.

In 1924 Nellie came down with a severe cold, which developed into pneumonia and sent her to a Fairbanks hospital. She was released within a few weeks, but she never fully recovered. The persistent ailment took its toll and contributed to the benevolent businesswoman's death. Nellie Cashman passed away on January 4, 1925.

Because Nellie had been so well known, newspapers in San Francisco, Tucson, Fairbanks, and Denver reported on the pioneer's death. Some called attention to her talent as a businesswoman and others highlighted her kind heart and nursing skills. The *Yukon Midnight Sun* in Dawson, Alaska, called Nellie the "miner's saint." They described her generous nature in glowing terms.

> She never wavered in her devotion to her church, and her faith in her chosen creed was absolute and unfaltering, and we may not doubt that, amid those lessening circles of latitude in her meditations upon the bright promise of immortality she some-times recognized a happy smile of the silent passing of the soul, in the unique splendors of the Arctic midnight sun when sunset merged into sunrise and a new day burst gloriously upon the page of time without even a shadow of farewell to the day that seemed not to have an end. Even so let us hope that to Nellie the pale shadow of death was but the weird drawing of the day eternal.

Nellie Cashman was buried next to her sister at Ross Bay Cemetery in Victoria, British Columbia. She was seventy-five years old. She is remembered in history books as a woman who possessed the unquenchable spirit of the Old West.

Pearl Hart

d. 1925 or 1955

"She flirted with the jury, bending them to her will."
— Judge Fletcher Dean after a jury
acquitted Pearl Hart of her crimes, 1900

Armed with a .44 Colt pistol and dressed in a man's gray flannel shirt, jeans, and boots, Pearl Hart rode off into the hills around Globe, Arizona, to rob an unsuspecting stagecoach. The petite twenty-eight-year-old woman had a cherublike face, short dark hair, and hard, penetrating little eyes. The white sombrero perched on her head was cocked to one side and cast a shadow over her small nose and plump cheeks.

While her accomplice seized the weapon the stage driver was carrying, Pearl lined the passengers alongside the road and relieved them of the more than $450 they possessed. Before the lady bandit sent the shaken travelers on their way, she provided them with one dollar. "That's for grub and lodging," she told them. Once the stage was off again, Pearl and her partner in crime rode out in the opposite direction.

The brazen daylight robbery that occurred on May 30, 1899, had historic significance. It was the last stage ever held up, and Pearl Hart was the last stage bandit, female or otherwise, to perpetrate such a crime. When news of the theft reached the public at large, Pearl became an overnight celebrity.

Born in Ontario, Canada, in 1871, Pearl was raised in a respectable middle-class family and attended the finest boarding schools in the town of Lindsay. Toward the end of her scholastic endeavors, she met the gambler Fredrick Hart and began a romantic relationship. Pearl was sixteen years old and the affair scandalized the school. The pair eloped in the spring of 1889.

The marriage was a volatile one from the start. Hart had a bad temper and drank a lot. He frequently took the losses he experienced at the poker table out on Pearl. The two argued constantly. During a trip to Chicago in 1893, the young bride managed to escape her abusive husband. She found work at the Wild West exhibition at the World's Columbian Exposition. She fell in love with her job and the history of the American West and its legends. Pearl was particularly enamored by the tales of highwaymen and road agents. She studied their tactics and dreamed of following in the footsteps of the James Gang.

In 1895 Hart caught up with his wife and begged her to forgive him. Pearl did, and the couple briefly reunited. Frederick worked as a bartender and hotel manager, and Pearl settled down to a life of domesticity. But after the birth of their second child, Hart returned to his old habits and started carousing, drinking too much, and abusing his wife. Pearl left him with her children in tow.

Now in her mid-twenties, Pearl traveled back to Canada, where she took on a series of odd jobs to support her family. Fascinated with the American West, she occasionally drifted to mining camps in Idaho, Montana, Colorado, and Arizona. In Benson, Arizona, she began seeing a miner named Joe Boot. Boot had a devil-may-care attitude and criminal tendencies Pearl found appealing. They discussed famous robberies and wondered aloud if they had the talent to pull off such crimes.

Brazen Pearl Hart served a five-year stretch in an Arizona prison for robbery and is known as the "last of the road agents."

A letter from Pearl's mother explaining that she was desperately ill and needed money to help purchase medicine reached her daughter in early 1899. Pearl tearfully shared her mother's dire situation with Boot, and he suggested they get the funds needed to assist her by robbing a stage.

There weren't many stages running in Arizona in the late 1890s; trains were now the primary means of transportation. Boot pointed out that a stage hadn't been robbed in some time and that no one would be expecting it to happen. She agreed, and the pair decided to over take the coach that ran from Florence to Globe. Joe had learned that the passengers were primarily businessmen who always traveled with large sums of money.

The holdup went smoothly, but their escape plan was fraught with complications. They got lost in the woods surrounding the crime scene and were eventually apprehended by a posse sent to arrest them. Pearl Hart and her cohort were charged with highway robbery, and their trial took place in Florence. News of Pearl's crime and the hearing were reported in newspapers throughout the country. For a while she was arguably the most famous woman in the world. The first jury found that the daring Mrs. Hart was a victim of circumstances and granted her an acquittal. The judge was furious with the verdict and ordered a second jury to be appointed. After warning them not to be swayed by the fact that she was a woman, the jury found her guilty. Pearl was then sentenced to five years in jail.

The bandit Pearl Hart served eighteen months of her sentence and was released on December 19, 1902. She left Arizona for Missouri and settled in Kansas City with her younger sister. The two wrote a play about Pearl's criminal exploits entitled *The Arizona Bandit*. The play closed after a handful of performances by the author herself.

There is some dispute over the date the famous lady thief

died. Some historians believe she passed away in 1925 in Kansas City. Others suggest she died in Arizona in 1955. The debate over the actual year of her death began with a courthouse clerk in Pima County, Arizona. According to the government employee, an elderly, feeble Pearl Hart visited the courthouse in 1925 and asked for a tour of the building. The clerk recognized the woman as the infamous bandit, and when he asked her if she was Pearl Hart she didn't deny it. Pearl informed the man that she had been tried and convicted of robbery in the courthouse and wanted to see the place again before she died. The clerk speculated that Pearl passed away shortly thereafter.

A newspaper writer conducting a census in the rural area around Globe, Arizona, reported that he interviewed Pearl at her home near the Christmas Mine outside Cane Springs in 1930. The spirited woman had married a rancher named Calvin Bywater and was living a peaceful life spent keeping a diary and tending to her garden. When he asked her where she had been born, she replied, "I wasn't born anywhere." After learning the reformed outlaw just wanted to be left alone and live out her days in quiet anonymity, he persuaded competing newspapers to leave her in peace. According to the same census taker, Pearl eventually died from complications of an addiction to morphine.

Pearl Hart's body lies in an unmarked grave in a small cemetery located at the base of the Dripping Springs Mountains near Globe.

Lillie Langtry
d. 1929

"I resent Mrs. Langtry. She has no right to be intelligent, daring and independent as well as lovely. It is a frightening combination of attributes."
— George Bernard Shaw, June 12, 1884

Twenty-three-year-old Lillie Langtry's striking looks inspired poets to write sonnets about her grace and pen-and-ink artists to sketch her elegant profile. She was known as a "Professional Beauty," one of a handful of women in England with such arresting features they were invited to the finest soirees just so guests could admire them. Langtry was a tall, curvaceous lady with titian red hair, and portraits of her sold in shops for a penny.

Emile Charlotte LeBreton was born to William Corbet and Emile Martin LeBreton in October 1853 on the Isle of Jersey, a few miles off the coast of Saint-Malo, France. She was the only daughter in a family of six children. Her mother called her "Lillie," which fit the beautiful child with lily-white skin.

Her education included studies in history, the classics, and early theater. By the time she turned age twenty, she had developed a love for theater and a strong desire to leave her birthplace and see the world she had read so much about.

*Emilie Charlotte LeBreton, better known as
Lillie Langtry, was America's first superstar.*

She married Edward Langtry on March 9, 1874, not long after watching his yacht sail into the Jersey harbor. He took her away from her home to England, where they met and mingled with the country's most renowned aristocrats. But their marriage would not survive the attention Lillie received from male admirers and friends who persuaded her to pursue a career on stage. The two separated after the birth of their daughter in April 1881.

Theater owners looking for a chance to capitalize on the well-known siren's popularity invited her to join their acting troupe. Knowing that only her beauty attracted them, Lillie refused all offers, deciding instead to take acting lessons. For months she trained with the critically acclaimed actress Henrietta Hodson Labouchere, and on December 15, 1881, she made her acting debut at the Theatre Royal in Westminster.

Lillie's performance was stunning, and audiences filled the house nightly. Labouchere became her manager and arranged for her pupil to appear at the most prestigious playhouses in England and Scotland. New York theater-owner and producer Henry Abbey saw Lillie in a show in Edinburgh and was instantly captivated by her talent. He wrote Labouchere with a generous proposal for Lillie, including an offer of 50 percent of the gross proceeds from her shows. Henrietta encouraged her student to accept, but Lillie held out for 65 percent of the gross and payment of all her travel expenses.

She set sail for America with assurance from her manager and producer that if she were successful in the United States, she could earn as much as a quarter of a million dollars on her first tour alone. Lillie's friend Oscar Wilde was on hand to meet her when she arrived in America. The day before he was to greet her, he told a newspaper reporter how much she meant to him: "I would rather have discovered Mrs. Langtry than to have discovered America. . . . It was for such as she that Troy was destroyed, and well it might have been."

Lillie Langtry's grave in Saint Saviour, Jersey,
is regularly visited by tourists and admirers.

Lillie's first tour of the United States was a huge triumph. Not only did she earn a quarter of a million dollars for the venture, but clothing manufacturers and makers of beverage and dry goods named their products after her. Songs and special waltzes were written for her. Her tour ended in March 1883, and she went back to England as one of the wealthiest actresses of the time.

After a brief return to England, she embarked on a second tour of the States. In April 1886 she traveled from the Atlantic to the Pacific and back again. She performed in numerous theaters in Texas, Colorado, Oregon, and California. Lillie traveled from one western town to the next in a private railcar designed especially for her by William Mann, the inventor and manufacturer of the sleeping car.

Lillie's personal life attracted as much attention as her professional one. The Jersey Lily (a nickname she acquired because of where she was born) was romantically linked to the Prince of Wales, gambler Diamond Jim Brady, and actor Maurice Barrymore. Articles about her scandalous romantic affairs appeared in newspaper and magazines alongside the complimentary reviews she received for her work. The enormous amount of attention paid to her love life never harmed her professional standing; if anything, it created longer lines at the box office.

At times Lillie's theatrical performances were upstaged by her beautiful costumes and dazzling jewelry. Critics claimed the clothing and gems made audiences forget the play, whereas Lillie maintained "sometimes diamonds were needed to bolster the material." Thousands of women bought seats in the hope that they would attend a performance in which Lillie wore her fabulous gems.

After another extended trip across the ocean to visit her family on the Isle of Jersey and to perform for the Queen of England, Lillie answered the call of the American public and returned to her adopted country in 1902, when she was fifty-one years old.

After touring in a pair of critically and financially successful plays and fully enjoying vaudeville life, Lillie announced her intentions to retire from the stage. In 1919 she gave up the theater, moved to a new home in Monaco, and plunged into the social whirl of the French Riviera's permanent residents. Her daughter and four grandchildren spent time with her there.

World-famous Lillie Langtry took ill in the fall of 1928. Her ailment was diagnosed as bronchitis complicated by pleurisy. She never completely recovered, and her weakened lungs were attacked again by a case of influenza. The actress died on February 12, 1929, at seventy-six years of age.

Owing to exhaustion and her desire for a quiet existence, Lillie lived the last five years of her life in almost complete solitude. She spent much of her time tending to her flower garden and had in her employ one household servant, Mrs. Peat, who was at the actress's side when she passed away.

Lillie's funeral was a small affair attended by only a few friends and family. Her relatives received letters of condolence from around the world, two of which came from King George V and Queen Mary.

Lillie Lantry was the first international celebrity of modern times. She left behind an estate valued at more than $230,000. She was buried next to her parents on the Isle of Jersey in the churchyard of St. Saviour's. Tourist and admirers regularly visit her magnificent marble grave.

Elizabeth Custer

d. 1933

"With my husband's departure my last days in the garrison were ended, as a premonition of disaster that I had never known before weighed me down."
—ELIZABETH BACON CUSTER, JUNE 24, 1876

She was known by the troops in General George A. Custer's command as the "Champion of the 7th." Many historians insist that there was no wife more devoted to her husband and or his work than Elizabeth Custer. The long-suffering widow was the first officer's wife to follow her spouse and his regiment into the field, and in so doing, she changed the image of army wives forever.

Prior to Elizabeth Custer's arrival on the scene, military wives were seldom if ever heard from, and in many circles, they were considered a distraction. Soldiers were encouraged to leave their spouses behind and never to discuss their careers with their wives. Elizabeth felt this was archaic: She believed a forceful, yet kindly presence in a husband's work could only enhance his career. Much of the career support George received from military leaders was due in part to Elizabeth as she charmed many senators, congressmen, and officers into backing the "boy general" and his lofty ambition of conquering the West.

Elizabeth Bacon Custer, 1842–1933

From the first days of their marriage during the Civil War, the Custers lived together in military encampments whenever possible. Separation, though often unavoidable, was agony. "It is infinitely worse to be left behind, a prey to all the horrors of imagining what may be happening to one we love," she recalled in one of her books, "My place is by my husband's side, wherever he may be."

Elizabeth Clift Bacon was born on April 18, 1842. She was one of four children born to Judge Daniel Bacon and his wife, Eleanor Sophia Page. Before Elizabeth had turned age eight, her siblings had died of cholera and other related diseases, leaving her an only child.

Daniel was quite protective of his daughter. He kept a close eye on all her activities. The older she got, the more beautiful she became. Eligible young men constantly sought her affections, but the judge was very particular about whom Elizabeth was able to see. He looked out not only for her physical safety but for her emotional well-being, too. When George Custer, an ambitious young soldier for the Union army, expressed an interest in Elizabeth, Daniel had strong objections. He thought Custer was too outspoken and brash for his genteel daughter. Like in many of these situations, these were the very qualities Elizabeth found appealing.

The unlikely pair met at a party in late November 1862. Elizabeth knew George by reputation, since he had achieved some distinction as an aide to General George McClellan. Custer was so smitten with Elizabeth that he walked up and down her street, hoping she would step out onto her porch so he could catch a glimpse of her. After a lengthy engagement the two were married in front of more than three hundred guests at the First Presbyterian Church in Monroe County, Michigan.

Elizabeth accompanied George in the field as often as she could and whenever it was reasonably safe to do so. Small and slender with delicate features, Mrs. Custer seemed physically unfit for life among the tents. Spiritually, she was up to the challenge. She found nontraditional camp life invigorating. From 1866 to 1873 the Custers were stationed at military posts throughout the plains. George was eventually named lieutenant colonel of the 7th Cavalry Regiment, and in 1873 he was ordered to the Dakota Territory to protect railway surveyors and gold miners who were crossing land owned by the Sioux. As she had done in the past, Elizabeth accompanied her husband to the unsettled region.

Some historians consider that Elizabeth's greatest contribution to army life was realized through her writing. She authored three books on the subject of life on the new frontier, describing momentous military events and providing readers with a detailed look at the Wild West. She also wrote about the heartbreaking moment George and his entire regiment were killed at the Battle of Little Bighorn. After being informed of his death on June 25, 1876, she accompanied the Fort Lincoln, Kansas, post commander as he made the rounds to break the news of the fatal incident to the other soldiers' wives. After several months of intense mourning, she managed to pull herself together and begin a new life without George. She visited the post hospital and helped care for the wounded men involved in similar skirmishes with the Indians. She prayed with them, read to them, and tended to their needs.

Elizabeth set her sights on living out her days as a hero's widow. Everywhere she went she was inundated with praise for George's legacy. A year after Custer's death, Elizabeth decided to begin work on a series of books about her life with the general. The first book was released in March 1885. With her third book, *Following the Guidon,* she firmly established George as a brilliant military commander and a devoted husband without personal failing.

Sixty-eight years after the death of her husband, Elizabeth Custer was lobbying Congress for a museum at the Little Bighorn

Battlefield. She believed the men who lost their lives in that conflict should be recognized for their heroism. Over the years she monitored the maintenance of the Custer Battlefield National Cemetery but was driven to create a more lasting memorial for the fallen soldiers. She never saw her dream realized.

Elizabeth Bacon Custer died of a heart attack two days before her ninety-first birthday in 1933. The estate she left behind to family, various charitable organizations, and Vassar College was estimated to be worth more than $100,000.

Per her request Elizabeth's funeral was a short service attended by only a handful of friends and members of the Custer family. She was buried next to her beloved husband at the U.S. Military Academy at West Point in New York. The flat stone that stands over her grave is minuscule, compared to the general's monument, and reads ELIZABETH CUSTER, WIFE OF GEORGE A. CUSTER.

Bibliography

Books

Aikman, Duncan. *Calamity Jane & the Lady Wildcats.* Lincoln: University of Nebraska Press, 1927.

Alexander, Kent. *Legends of the Old West.* New York: Friedman/Fairfax Publishers, 1994.

Bakeless, John. *Spies of the Confederacy.* Mineola, N.Y.: Dover Publications, 1970.

Banks, Leo. *Stalwart Women.* Phoenix: Arizona Highways, 1999.

Beebe, Lucius, and Charles Clegg. *The American West.* New York: E. P. Dutton & Company, 1955.

Boyer, Glenn. *Wyatt Earp–Family, Friends & Foes.* Rodeo, N. Mex.: Historical Research Associates, 1997.

Brown, Dee. *Gentle Tamers: Women of the Old Wild West.* Lincoln: University of Nebraska Press, 1958.

———. *Showdown at Little Big Horn.* Lincoln: University of Nebraska Press, 1964.

———. *The Westerners.* New York: Holt, Rinehart & Winston, 1974.

———. *Wondrous Times on the Frontier.* New York: Harper Perennial, 1992.

Bryan, Howard. *Wildest of the Wild West.* Santa Fe, N. Mex.: Clear Light Publishing, 1988.

Byrne, Robert. *The 2,548 Best Things Anybody Ever Said*. New York: Galahad Books, 1996.

Chartier, JoAnn, and Chris Enss. *Gilded Girls*. Guilford, Conn.: Globe Pequot Press, 2003.

————. *Love Untamed*. Guilford, Conn.: Globe Pequot Press, 2002.

————. *She Wore a Yellow Ribbon*. Guilford, Conn.: Globe Pequot Press, 2004.

————. *With Great Hope*. Guilford, Conn.: Globe Pequot Press, 2000.

Curry, Peggy S. *The Women Who Made the West*. New York: A Discus Book, 1980.

Fiske, Jack. *Big Nose Kate*. Tombstone, Ariz.: American Serials, 1997.

Fitzhenry, Robert I. *The Harper Book of Quotations*. New York: Harper Perennial, 1993.

Florin, Lambert. *Historic Graves of the Old West*. New York: Bonanza Books, 1958.

Forbes, Malcolm. *They Went That-A-Way*. New York: Ballantine Books, 1988.

Forbis, William H., and the editors of Time-Life Books. *The Cowboys*. Alexandria, Va.: Time-Life Books, 1973.

Furbee, Mary R. *Outrageous Women of the American Frontier*. New York: John Wiley & Sons, Inc., 2002.

Horn, Huston, and the editors of Time-Life Books. *The Pioneers*. Alexandria, Va.: Time-Life Books, 1974.

Lardner, W. B., and M. J. Brock. *History of Placer and Nevada Counties, California*. Los Angeles: Historical Record Company, 1924.

Leckie, Shirley. *Elizabeth Bacon Custer*. Norman: University of Oklahoma Press, 1993.

Loose, Warren. *Bodie Bonanza*. Las Vegas: Nevada Publications, 1989.

Luchetti, Cathy, and Carol Olwell. *Women of the West*. New York: Crown Trade Paperback, 1982.

MacKell, Jan. *Prostitution in Colorado*. Albuquerque: University of New Mexico Press, 2004.

McDonald, Douglas. *The Legend of Julia Bulette*. Las Vegas: Stanley Paher Publishing, 1980.

McNeer, May. *The California Gold Rush*. New York: Random House, 1950.

Miller, R., and Hanna C Miller. *The Story of Stagecoach Mary Fields*. Denver: Silver Press, 1994.

Nash, Jay R. *Encyclopedia of Western Lawmen & Outlaws*. New York: Paragon House, 1989.

Nevin, David, and the editors of Time-Life Books. *The Expressman*. Alexandria, Va.: Time-Life Books, 1974.

———. *The Soldiers*. Alexandria, Va.: Time-Life Books, 1973.

Reiter, Joan Swallow, and the editors of Time-Life Books. *The Women*. Alexandria, Va.: Time-Life Books, 1978.

Rezatto, Helen. *Tales of the Black Hills*. Rapid City, S. Dak.: Fenwyn Press, 1989.

Russell, Jerry. *176 Facts about Custer & the Battle of Little Big Horn*. Cambridge, Mass.: DA Capo Press, 1999.

Seagraves, Anne. *Women of the Sierra*. Lakeport, Calif.: Wesanne Enterprises, 1990.

———. *Women Who Charmed the West*. Lakeport, Calif.: Wesanne Enterprises, 1991.

Selcer, Richard. *Hell's Half Acre*. Fort Worth: Texas Christian University Press, 1991.

Sheafer, Silvia Anne. *Frontier Women*. Glendale, Calif.: Historical California Press, 1992.

Trachtman, Paul, and the editors of Time-Life Books. *The Gunfighters*. Alexandria, Va.: Time-Life Books, 1974.

Utley, Robert M. *Custer Battlefield*. Washington, D.C.: National Parks Service, 1969.

Vestal, Stanley. *Jim Bridger, Mountain Man*. Lincoln: University of Nebraska, 1970.

Virgines, George. *The Arizona Rangers*. New York: Colt Industries, Firearms Division, 1972.

Wallace, Robert, and the editors of Time-Life Books. *The Miners*. Alexandria, Va.: Time-Life Books, 1976.

Ward, Geoffery. *The West*. New York: Little Brown & Company, 1996.

Wheeler, Kurt, and the editors of Time-Life Books. *The Townsmen*. Alexandria, Va.: Time-Life Books, 1975.

Williams, George III. *The Red Light Ladies of Virginia City, Nevada*. Riverside, Calif.: Tree by the River Publishing, 1984.

Zauner, Phyllis. *Those Legendary Men of the Wild West*. Sonoma, Calif.: Zanel Publications, 1998.

———. *Those Spirited Women of the Early West*. Sonoma, Calif.: Zanel Publications, 1994.

About the Author

Chris Enss is an award-winning screen writer who has written for television, short subject films, live performances, and for the movies. Her research and writing and reveals the funny, touching, exciting, and tragic stories of historical and contemporary times.

Enss has done everything from stand-up comedy to working as a stunt person at the Old Tucson Movie Studio. She learned the basics of writing for film and television at the University of Arizona, and she is currently working with *Return of the Jedi* producer Howard Kazanjian on the movie version of *The Cowboy and the Senorita,* their biography of western stars Roy Rogers and Dale Evans.

Other Books by Chris Enss

Frontier Teachers: Stories of Heroic Women of the Old West

A Beautiful Mine: Women PRospectors of the Old West

*Outlaw Tales of California: True Stories of the Golden Steve's Most
    Infamous Crooks, Culprits, and Cutthorats*

The Lady Was a Gambler: True Stories of Notorious Women of the Old West

*Tales Behind Tombstones: The Deaths and Burials of the Old West's Most
    Nefarious Outlaws, Notorious Women, and Celebrated Lawmen*

Pistol Packin' Madams: True Stories of Notorious Women of the Old West

The Doctor Wore Petticoats: Women Physicians of the Old West

Buffalo Gals: Women of Buffalo Bill's Wild West Show

How the West Was Worn: Bustles and Buckskins on the Wild Frontier

Hearts West: True Stories of Mail-Order Brides on the Frontier

With Howard Kazanjian

The Young Duke: The Early Life of John Wayne

*Happy Trails: A Pictorial Celebration of the Life and Times of Roy Rogers
    and Dale Evans*

The Cowboy and the Senorita: A Biography of Roy Rogers and Dale Evans

With JoAnn Chartier

With Great Hope: Women of the California Gold Rush

Love Untamed: Romances of the Old West

Gilded Girls: Women Entertainers of the Old West

*She Wore a Yellow Ribbon: Women Soldiers and Patriots of the
    Western Frontier*